RANDOM HOUSE

HOUSE

LARGE
PRINT

HAPPINESS
IN THIS
LIFE

Also by Pope Francis
Available from Random House Large Print

The Name of God Is Mercy

POPE FRANCIS

HAPPINESS IN THIS LIFE

A Passionate Meditation
on Earthly Existence

Translated from the Italian
by Oonagh Stransky

RANDOM HOUSE
LARGE PRINT

Copyright © 2017 by
Edizione Piemme Spa, Milano
Copyright © 2017 by
Libreria Editrice Vaticana, Città del Vaticano
English translation copyright © 2017 by
Penguin Random House LLC

All rights reserved.
Published in the United States of America by
Random House Large Print in association with
Random House, an imprint and division of
Penguin Random House LLC, New York.

Cover design by Nick Misani
Cover photograph © Franco Origlia/
Getty Images

ISBN: 978-0-5256-3158-3

www.randomhouse.com/largeprint

FIRST LARGE PRINT EDITION

Printed in the United States of America

10 9 8 7 6 5 4 3 2 1

This Large Print edition published in accord
with the standards of the N.A.V.H.

CONTENTS

Introduction: The Path of Happiness   ix

PART I
YOUR SEARCH FOR A MEANINGFUL LIFE

Dreams and Plans for the Future   3
The Secret of Life   50
Free and Liberated People   98

PART II
YOU AND OTHERS:
HAPPINESS IN YOUR RELATIONSHIPS

Let Your Light Be Contagious   117
The Family, Life's Bounty   154
Successful Lives: When the Lord's Call
Is Answered with Joy   177
The Blessings and Challenges
of Womanhood   202

PART III
A HUNDREDFOLD REWARD—
PLUS SUFFERING

Beyond Tears and Loneliness 223
From Errors to Forgiveness 265
A Hundred Eternities 288

PART IV
THEY WHO PRAY LIVE SERENELY

Prayer Completes Us 323
Pope Francis's Prayers for
a Fulfilling Life 335

Introduction
THE PATH OF HAPPINESS

The Beatitudes are God's response to man's innate desire for happiness, and they complement the Commandments of the Old Testament. We are accustomed to learning the Ten Commandments—of course you know them, you learned them in Sunday school!—but we are not used to memorizing the Beatitudes. Let us try to remember them and imprint them upon our hearts.

First: "Blessed are the poor in spirit, for theirs is the Kingdom of Heaven."

"Blessed are they who mourn, for they will be comforted."

"Blessed are the meek, for they will inherit the land."

"Blessed are they who hunger and thirst for righteousness, for they will be satisfied."

"Blessed are the merciful, for they will be shown mercy."

"Blessed are the clean of heart, for they will see God."

"Blessed are the peacemakers, for they will be called children of God."

"Blessed are they who are persecuted for the sake of righteousness, for theirs is the Kingdom of Heaven."

"Blessed are you when they insult you and persecute you and utter every kind of evil against you falsely because of Me."

"Rejoice and be glad, for your reward will be great in Heaven. Thus they persecuted the prophets who were before you."

Take the Gospel, the one you carry with you—remember that you should always carry a little Gospel with you, in your pocket or purse. Always. The Beatitudes are found in chapter 5 of Matthew. Read them every day, try not to forget them. They are the Law that Jesus gives us!

These words contain all of Christ's Gospel: All of Christ's Gospel is found in these words. In fact, the Beatitudes are the essence of Jesus, His way of life; and they are the path to true happiness, which we, too, can travel with the grace that Jesus gives us.

General Audience, August 6, 2014

HAPPINESS
IN THIS
LIFE

PART I

YOUR SEARCH FOR A
MEANINGFUL LIFE

Dreams and Plans for the Future

With Christ, joy is
constantly born anew.
EVANGELII GAUDIUM

THE GOSPEL OF
A FULFILLED LIFE

—

The joy of the Gospel fills the hearts
and lives of all who encounter Jesus.
Those who accept His salvation are
freed from sin, sorrow, emptiness, and
loneliness.

Evangelii Gaudium 1

THE GREAT QUESTION: IS HOPE POSSIBLE, HERE AND NOW?

—

The **frantic pace** of modern life seems to steal away all hope and joy from our daily lives. The pressures and the powerlessness we experience in so many situations seem to shrivel our souls; the countless challenges we face stupefy us, paralyze us. The world is speeding up to build—in theory—a better society, yet paradoxically at the end of the day there is no time for anything or for anyone. We have no time to spend with our families or our communities, no time for friendship, for consensus, or for reflection.

We should ask ourselves: How can we enact the joy of the Gospel in our daily lives, in our cities? Is Christian hope possible, here and now?

These two questions shape our identity, the lives of our families, our towns, and our cities.

Homily, March 25, 2017

A SALAD WITH OIL . . .

—

Jesus had just finished speaking about the dangers of wealth, and about how difficult it was for a rich man to enter the Kingdom of Heaven. Peter asked Him, "We have left everything and followed You. What do we get in return?" Jesus was generous with Peter. He said, "Truthfully, I will say this: Everyone who left their homes or brothers or sisters or mothers or fathers or fields for My cause or for the Gospel will receive in return a hundredfold . . ."

Peter probably thought, "This is good business, then, if I follow Jesus I will earn a hundredfold!" But then Jesus added three small words: "along with persecution." Yes, you will have eternal life. Yes, you left everything behind. Yes, you will receive many things here on earth as well. But you will also be persecuted.

It's like salad, served with the oil of

persecution. This is a Christian's reward. **This** is the path that a person who follows Jesus has to take. Because this is the path that He took: He, too, was persecuted.

Homily at Casa Santa Marta,
June 9, 2014

OPEN YOUR HEART TO THE KINGDOM OF GOD

In the parables, Jesus tells us that the Kingdom comes into the world humbly, growing silently yet surely wherever it is welcomed by hearts open to its message of hope and salvation. The Gospel teaches us that the Spirit of Jesus can bring new life to every human heart and can transform any situation, even apparently hopeless ones. Jesus can change everything! This is the message that you are called on to share with the people around you: at school, in the workplace, in your families, in your universities and your communities. Because Jesus rose from the dead, we know that He has "the words of eternal life" (John 6:68), that His Word has the power to touch every heart, to conquer evil, and to change and redeem the world.

Address, August 15, 2014

How are you? Are you happy?
—

As Saint Paul wrote: "Rejoice in the Lord always . . . The Lord is near" (Philippians 4:4–5). Today I would like to ask you all a question. But you need to keep the question in your heart and take it home with you, as a kind of homework. And you have to do your homework on your own. Is there joy in your home? Is there joy in your family? That's the question you have to answer.

Dear families, you know very well that the true joy we experience within a family is not superficial; it does not come from material things, or from the fact that everything seems to be going well . . . True joy comes from a profound harmony among people, something that we feel in our hearts and that lets us experience the beauty of togetherness, of mutual support along life's journey. This feeling of deep joy is rooted in God, the presence of God in the family, and His love, which is welcoming, merciful, and respectful toward all. Above all, this love is patient. Patience is a virtue of God and we must cultivate it in family life, and learn to have this patient love for one another. To be patient with one another. A patient love. God alone knows how to create harmony out of differences. If God's love is lacking, the family loses its harmony, individualism prevails, and joy fades. But the family that experiences the joy of faith communicates that joy naturally; joy is the salt of the earth and the light of the world. It is the yeast that leavens society as a whole.

Homily, October 27, 2013

Don't stifle your dreams

I wish to state this clearly to the young, whose freshness and optimism make them openhearted and generous. At times, uncertainty, worries about the future, and daily problems may risk paralyzing your youthful enthusiasm and shattering your dreams. You may not think that your dreams are worth the effort. You may think that the God of the Christian faith somehow limits your freedom. Dear young friends, never be afraid to attempt the journey, to venture outside yourselves! The Gospel is the Word; it liberates, transforms, and makes our lives all the more beautiful.

Message for World Day of Prayer for Vocations, March 29, 2015

Do you feel unfulfilled? Let yourself be embraced by God

—

We often fail to see God's plan. We often realize that we cannot ensure our own happiness and eternal life. However, it is precisely when we experience our own limitations and weaknesses that the Holy Spirit comforts us. Our weaknesses help us understand what is most important: We must allow Jesus to lead us into His Father's arms.

General Audience, June 11, 2014

The path of the saints (and you)

—

If there is one thing that characterizes the saints, it is that they are genuinely **happy**. They discovered the secret of true happiness, a happiness that lives deep within the soul and whose source is the love of God. This is why we call the saints blessed.

Homily, November 1, 2016

GOD COMFORTS YOU
LIKE A MOTHER
—

In the same way that a mother takes up the burdens and weariness of her children, so, too, does God take upon Himself our sins and troubles. He knows us and loves us infinitely. He is mindful of our prayers and He wipes away our tears. He looks at us with innate love; He is moved by us; He becomes tenderhearted. We will always be His children, no matter how badly we may act. He wants to take us in His arms, protect us, and free us from harm and evil. Let us allow these words of the Lord to echo in our hearts: "Like a mother, I will comfort you."

Homily, October 1, 2016

THE IMAGE OF CHRIST COMPLETES YOU

—

A believer learns to see himself through the faith he professes. The image of Christ is the mirror through which a believer discovers his true self. And just as Christ embraces all those who believe, making them His body, so the Christian who sees himself as a part of this body understands his essential relationship with Christ and his brothers in faith.

Lumen Fidei 22

BE LIKE A CHILD IN THE EMBRACE OF THE HOLY SPIRIT

—

When the Holy Spirit dwells in our hearts, we feel comfort and peace. We understand how small we are. We experience the feeling—a feeling so strongly recommended by Jesus in the Gospel—of placing all our cares and hopes in God and being embraced and sustained by His warmth and protection, just like a child with his dad! This is what the Holy Spirit does to our hearts: It makes us feel like children in the arms of our dad. In this way, we understand how fear of the Lord can become docility, gratitude, and praise, and how it fills our hearts with hope.

General Audience, June 11, 2014

I WANT A LOVE THAT LASTS FOREVER

—

The human heart aspires to great things, lofty values, deep friendships, ties that are strengthened by the trials of life rather than broken by them. People long to love and to be loved in return. Love is our clearest and deepest aspiration: to love and be loved. But the "culture of the temporary" does not honor our freedom, it deprives us of our true destiny, of our truest and most authentic goals. It creates a fragmented life. It is sad to reach a certain age, to look over the journey we have made and find that it was made up of scraps, without unity, without form: everything temporary . . .

Address, July 5, 2014

IN AN ERA OF ORPHANHOOD, YOU HAVE A FATHER

—

God is not a distant and anonymous being. He is our refuge, the source of peace and serenity. He is the rock of our salvation, to which we can cling with certainty. One who clings to God never falls! He is our defense against ever-lurking evil. God is a great friend, an ally, and a father, but we do not always realize it. We do not realize that we have a friend, an ally, and a father who loves us. Instead we prefer to rely on material goods, things that we can touch, forgetting and at times rejecting the supreme good, which is the paternal love of God. To know and feel that we have a father in this era of orphanhood is so important!

Angelus, February 26, 2017

I JUST CAN'T DO IT . . .

—

We can't do it alone. Confronted with the pressures of everyday life, we are rarely able to find the right path on our own—and even when we do, we may lack the strength to persevere, to face the climb and the unexpected obstacles along the way. And this is where the Lord Jesus's invitation comes in: "If you want . . . follow Me." He offers to accompany us on our journey—not to exhaust us, not to make slaves of us, but to free us. He asks us to join Him: That's it, to join Him. Only by joining Jesus, by praying to Jesus and following

Him, do we find the clarity of vision and strength to go forward. He loves us; He has chosen us; He gave Himself to each one of us. He is our defender and big brother and will be our only judge. How beautiful it is to be able to face life's ups and downs in the company of Jesus, to have His person and His message with us! He does not take away autonomy or liberty; on the contrary, by fortifying our fragility, He permits us to be truly free. He gives us the freedom to do good and the strength to continue doing so; He makes us capable of forgiving and capable of asking for forgiveness. This is the Jesus who accompanies us. This is the Lord!

Address, July 5, 2014

Don't be withdrawn, don't get overwhelmed, don't become a prisoner

—

Don't be withdrawn, don't get overwhelmed by everyday problems, don't become a prisoner of your own troubles. They will be resolved if you go forth, help others resolve their problems, and proclaim the Good News. You will find life by giving life, hope by giving hope, love by loving.

Letter to All Consecrated People,
November 21, 2014

Go forth: You will reap a hundred times more

—

At the root of every Christian vocation is the moving experience of faith. Believing means transcending ourselves, leaving behind our comforts and the inflexibility of our egos in order to put Jesus Christ at the center of our lives.

It means leaving our native place and going forth with trust, knowing that God will show us the way to a new land, as He did with Abraham. This "going forth" shouldn't be seen as a sign of dissatisfaction with your life, your feelings, or your humanity. On the contrary, those who set out to follow Christ find life in abundance by putting themselves completely at the service of God and His Kingdom. Jesus says: "Everyone who has given up houses or brothers or sisters or father or mother or children or lands for the sake of My name will receive a hundred times more, and will inherit eternal life" (Matthew 19:29). "Going forth" has its roots in love.

Message for World Day of Prayer for Vocations, March 29, 2015

BREAK DOWN THE BARRIERS
OF FEAR
—

"Hail, favored one! The Lord is with you" (Luke 1:28). These were the first words that the Archangel Gabriel addressed to the Virgin. When someone finds Jesus, their life is filled with an inner joy so great that nothing and no one can take it away. When problems seem insurmountable, Christ gives His believers the strength to be neither sad nor disheartened. A Christian is upheld by this truth; he knows that his loving actions generate serene joy, and that this joy, which is the sister of hope, breaks down the barriers of fear and opens the door to a promising future.

Message, September 8, 2014

DON'T SETTLE FOR A SMALL LIFE

—

Do you really want to be happy? In an age when we are constantly being tempted by vain and empty illusions of happiness, we risk settling for less and living "small." Instead: Think big! Open your heart! As Blessed Pier Giorgio Frassati once said, "To live without faith, to have no heritage to uphold, to fail to struggle constantly to defend the truth: This is not living, it is getting by. We should never just get by, but really live" (**Letter to I. Bonini,** February 27, 1925).

Message for World Youth Day,
January 21, 2014

LET THE SPIRIT OPEN YOUR HEART

—

This is why we need the gift of the Holy Spirit: Fear of the Lord makes us aware that everything comes from

grace. Our true strength lies in following the Lord Jesus, allowing the Father
to bestow upon us His goodness and
His mercy, and opening our hearts so
that the goodness and the mercy of
God may come to us. This is what the
Holy Spirit does through the gift of fear
of the Lord: He opens hearts. The heart
opens so that forgiveness, mercy, goodness, and the caress of the Father may
come to us. For we are His infinitely
loved children.

General Audience, June 11, 2014

TODAY TAKES COURAGE

Today is a time for action and a time
for courage! We need courage to steady
our wavering steps, to recapture the enthusiasm of devoting ourselves to the
Gospel, to recover confidence in our
mission and the strength it brings. This
is a time for courage, although courage
alone does not guarantee success. We

need courage in order to fight, but not to win; in order to proclaim, but not necessarily to convert. We need courage to find alternatives, without ever becoming polemical or aggressive. We must have courage in order to open ourselves up to the world, diminishing neither the wholeness nor the uniqueness of Christ the Savior. Courage is required in order to resist skepticism, yet without becoming arrogant. Today we must have the courage of the tax collector in the Gospel, who humbly did not dare even to raise his eyes to Heaven, but beat his breast saying: "God, be merciful to me, a sinner!" Today is a day for courage! Today, courage is needed!

Angelus, October 23, 2016

GOD IN OUR HEARTS

—

To face the turmoil we experience in life, we need the presence of God in our hearts. His presence in us is the source of true consolation: It stays with us, it frees us from evil, it brings peace, and it increases our joy.

Homily, October 1, 2016

WHO ANNOYS POPE FRANCIS?

—

When I hear a young person or a Sunday school teacher or anyone, really, speaking drearily about the Lord, I get annoyed. We talk about the Lord with such sadness. He said **joy**! That's the secret. Let's talk about the Lord with **joy**; this is what it means to bear witness as a Christian. Do you understand?

Meeting with Children and Young People, January 15, 2017

BE A PERSON WHO SINGS A SONG OF LIFE

—

Be a person who sings a song of life, who sings a song of faith. It is important not only to recite the Creed and to act with faith and to understand the faith, but to **sing** the faith! That's it! Talk about faith and live faith with joy; that is "singing the faith." And I didn't invent this! Sixteen hundred years ago, Saint Augustine said, "Sing a song of faith!"

Address, May 3, 2014

THE DISTILLERY OF FEAR

—

It is easier to believe in a ghost than in the living Christ! It is easier to go to a fortune-teller who predicts the future and reads your cards than to have faith in the hope of a victorious Christ, in a Christ who triumphed over death! It is easier to have an idea or imagine something than to give yourself meekly to this Lord who rose from the dead and wait to find out what He might have in store for you! This habit of making our faith relative ends up distancing us from the encounter and removing us from God's caress. It's as if we "distill" the reality of Jesus Christ out of fear, sublimate it out of a wish for safety, because we want to control the encounter ourselves. The disciples were afraid of joy . . . and so are we.

Homily, April 24, 2014

HAPPINESS CAN'T BE BOUGHT

Happiness can't be bought. And whenever you try to buy happiness, you soon realize that it has vanished. The happiness you can buy does not last. Only the happiness of love lasts!

The path of love is simple: Love God and love your neighbor, love your brother or sister, love whoever is near you and whoever needs love or needs anything else. "But, Father, how do I know that I love God?" It's easy. If you love your neighbor, if you do not have hatred in your heart, you love God. That is the ultimate test.

Address, August 15, 2014

Do you want to leave, too?

Jesus challenges us to take His approach to life seriously and to decide which path is right for us, which way will lead to true joy. This is the great challenge of faith. Jesus was not afraid to ask His disciples if they genuinely wanted to follow Him or if they preferred to take another path (John 6:67). Simon Peter had the courage to reply: "Master, to whom shall we go? You have the words of eternal life" (John 6:68). If you can say yes to Jesus, your lives will become both meaningful and fruitful.

Message for World Youth Day,
January 21, 2014

LOOK AT YOUR TALENTS, LOOK AT YOUR LIMITS: YOU ARE NOT ALONE!

—

Be someone who knows how to recognize both your talents and your limits. Be someone who knows how to see—even in your darkest days—the signs of the Lord's presence. Rejoice because the Lord has called you to share in the mission of His Church. Rejoice because you are not alone on this journey. You have the Lord; He is with you. You have your bishops and priests who sustain you. You have your parish communities and your diocesan communities with whom you can share the journey. You are not alone!

Address, May 3, 2014

FACE LIFE WITH STRENGTH AND DON'T GIVE UP

—

It is sad to see young people who "have everything" but are weak. Saint John, writing to young people, said: "You are strong, and the Word of God remains in you, and you have conquered the Evil One" (1 John 2:14). Young people who choose Christ **are** strong: They are fed by His Word and don't need to "stuff themselves" with other things! Have the courage to go against the grain. Have the courage to be truly happy! Say no to an ephemeral, superficial, throwaway culture, a culture that assumes that you are incapable of taking on responsibility and facing the great challenges of life!

Message for World Youth Day,
January 21, 2014

NEVER BE AFRAID TO TAKE
THE RISK OF BEING HAPPY

—

In the Gospel passage we just heard, the disciples could not believe the joy they felt, because they could not believe in the cause of this joy. This is what the Gospel tells us. Let's revisit the scene: Jesus has risen and the disciples of Emmaus are speaking about their experience. Peter is also telling what he saw. Then the Lord appears in the room and says to them: "Peace be with you." Many feelings erupt in the hearts of the disciples: fear, surprise, doubt, and, finally, joy. A joy so great that they "could not believe it." They were amazed—stunned—and Jesus, almost with a faint smile, asks them for something to eat and starts explaining the Scriptures, opening their minds so they can understand. This is the moment of astonishment, of the encounter with Jesus Christ, a moment of such joy that it feels like a dream, an illusion. In such moments we are tempted to take shelter in skepticism, to "not exaggerate," because joy and happiness feel risky.

Homily, April 24, 2014

JESUS'S CHOICE IS OUR FREEDOM

When He became poor, Jesus did not seek poverty for its own sake but, as Saint Paul says, "that by His poverty you might become rich." This is not a play on words or a catchphrase! Rather, it sums up God's logic, the logic of love, the logic of the Incarnation and the Cross. God did not simply hand out salvation like someone giving money to a beggar because they have extra change, or because they want to feel pious and philanthropic. Christ's love is different! Jesus steps into the waters of the Jordan and is baptized by John the Baptist not because He is in need of repentance or conversion. He did it to be among people who need forgiveness—among us sinners—and to take the burden of our sins upon Himself. This is how He chose to comfort us, to save us, and to free us from our misery.

Message for Lent, 2014

ALL TOGETHER NOW: JOY IS AT HOME IN JESUS!

Jesus came in order to bring joy to all people for all time. This joy is not a question of hope, or something that awaits us in Paradise, as if we are sad here on earth but we will be filled with joy in Paradise. No! This joy is real and tangible now, because Jesus Himself is our joy, and with Jesus joy finds its home, as your sign there says: JOY IS AT HOME IN JESUS. All of us, let us say it: "Joy is at home in Jesus." Once more: "Joy is at home in Jesus." And is there joy without Jesus? No! Well done! He is living, He is the Risen One, and He works in us and among us especially with the Word and the Sacraments.

Angelus, December 14, 2014

Come to Me, YOU WHO ARE TIRED!

—

As Jesus says in the Gospel of Matthew: "Come to Me, all you who labor and are burdened, and I will give you rest" (Matthew 11:28). Life is often tiring, and often tragically so! . . . Work is exhausting, looking for work is exhausting; even finding work today requires so much effort! But what is most burdensome in life, what drags us down most, is the absence of love. It weighs on us if we never receive a smile, if we never receive a warm welcome. Certain silences weigh on us, like those in families, between husbands and wives, between parents and children, among siblings.

Without love, our exhaustion becomes even heavier; it becomes intolerable. I think of elderly people living alone, and families who receive no help in caring for someone at home with special needs. "Come to Me, all you who labor and are burdened," Jesus says.

Address, October 26, 2013

SOURCE, MANIFESTATION, SOUL

—

The Father is the source of joy; the Son is the manifestation of joy; and the Holy Spirit is its catalyst, its animating force, its spark. Immediately after praising the Father, as the evangelist Matthew tells us, Jesus says: "Come to me, all you who labor and are burdened, and I will give you rest. Take My yoke upon you and learn from Me, for I am meek and humble of heart, and you will find rest for yourselves. For My yoke is easy, and My burden light" (Matthew 11:28–30). "The joy of the

Gospel fills the hearts and lives of all who encounter Jesus. Those who accept His salvation are freed from sin, sorrow, emptiness, and loneliness. With Christ joy is constantly born anew" (**Evangelii Gaudium** 1).

The Virgin Mary had a unique encounter with Jesus and subsequently became **causa nostrae laetitiae** (Latin: the cause of our joy). The disciples, for their part, received the call to follow Jesus and were sent by Him to preach the Gospel, and they were filled with joy. Why shouldn't we step into this river of joy, too?

Message, June 8, 2014

LEAVE YOUR AMPHORA

In the Gospel passage of the Samaritan we find the impetus to "leave behind our amphora," the water jar, the symbol of everything that is seemingly important but that loses all value in the face of the love of God. We all have one, or more than one! I ask you—and I ask myself, too!—"What is your inner amphora, the thing that weighs you down, that distances you from God?" Let us set it aside and with our hearts listen to the voice of Jesus offering us another kind of water, the kind of water that brings us close to the Lord. We are called on to rediscover the importance and the essence of our Christian life, which begins with Baptism and asks that we bear witness to our brothers, like the Samaritan woman. To bear witness to what? To joy! We are called on to speak of the joy of our encounter with Jesus. For, as I said, every encounter with Jesus changes our life, and every encounter with Jesus fills us with joy, a joy that comes from within. That's the way the Lord is. And so we can speak of the marvelous things the Lord can do in our hearts—when we have the courage to set aside our own amphorae.

Angelus, March 13, 2014

GO FORTH AND LOOK FOR LIGHT

If you want to see the light you must go forth, you need to go outside yourself and look for it. You can't be withdrawn and just watch what is going on around you. You have to put your own life at stake and go forth. A Christian life is a **continuous journey** made of hope, a quest; it is a journey like that of the Magi, which continues even when the star momentarily disappears from view. There are dangers on this journey, dangers that should be avoided: Superficial and mundane gossip slows down the pace; selfish whims are paralyzing; and the pit of pessimism traps all hope.

Angelus, January 6, 2017

DON'T BE CONTENT
WITH SMALL GOALS

—

Do not rob yourself of the desire to build great and lasting things in your life! This ambition is what takes you forward. Do not content yourselves with small goals! Aspire to happiness, have courage: the courage to go outside yourselves and to stake everything on your future with Jesus.

Address, July 5, 2014

RESIST "BARGAIN" OFFERS

—

If you allow your deepest, most heartfelt aspirations to emerge, you will realize that you possess an incorruptible desire for happiness. This yearning will allow you to expose and reject the real cost of the many "bargains" you are offered. When we search for success and pleasure through possessions or egotism, when we worship these false idols, we may well have moments of exhilaration and feel a fleeting sense of satisfaction. Ultimately, however, we become enslaved; we are never satisfied and always look for more.

Message for World Youth Day,
January 21, 2014

THE JOY OF GOD IS THE PRESENCE OF JESUS AMONG US

On the third Sunday of Lent, the Liturgy suggests another mindset to help us await the Lord: joy. That's it—the Liturgy talks about Jesus's joy!

The human heart desires joy. We all desire joy. Every family, every individual aspires to happiness. But what is the joy that the Christian is called to live out and bear witness to? It is the joy that comes from the closeness of God, from His **presence** in our life. From the moment Jesus entered history, with His birth in Bethlehem, humanity received the seed of the Kingdom of God, as the soil receives the seed and the promise of a future harvest. There is no need to look anywhere else!

Angelus, December 14, 2014

LOVE BEAUTY, SEARCH FOR TRUTH

—

[In response to the question "When I read the newspapers, when I look around, I wonder if the human race is really capable of taking care of this world and of the human race itself. Do you also feel this doubt sometimes, do you doubt and say: But where is God in all this?"] For me, a young person who loves truth and looks for it, someone who loves goodness and is good, who is a good person, someone who looks for and loves inner beauty, is on the right track and will find God for sure! Sooner or later he or she will find Him! But the road is long, and some people don't find Him in their lifetime. They don't find Him consciously. But they themselves are so true and honest, so good, and such lovers of inner beauty, that at the end they have a very mature personality, a personality capable of an encounter with God, which is always a grace. Because an encounter with God is grace.

We can build the road. Some people find Him in other people . . . It is a road worth building. Everyone must find Him in his or her own way. God cannot be found through hearsay, nor can you pay to encounter Him. It is a personal journey, and we must meet Him personally. I don't know if I answered your question . . .

Meeting with Young People,
March 31, 2014

A SCENE FULL OF LIGHT

Jesus enters Jerusalem. The crowd of disciples accompanies Him in a festive mood, they have laid out their cloaks along the path before Him, there is talk of the miracles He has accomplished, and loud praises are heard: "Blessed is the king who comes in the name of the Lord. Peace in Heaven and glory in the highest" (Luke 19:38).

Crowds celebrating, praises, blessings, peace; joy fills the air, you can almost breathe it in. Jesus has awakened great hopes, especially in the hearts of the simple, the humble, the poor, the forgotten, those who do not matter in the eyes of the world. He has shown that He understands human misery, He has shown the face of God's mercy, and He has bent down to heal body and soul.

This is Jesus. This is His heart, which sees every one of us, through our sicknesses, through our sins. The love of

Jesus is great. And thus He enters Jerusalem, with this love, and looks at us all. It is a beautiful scene, full of light—the light of the love of Jesus, the love of His heart—of joy, of celebration.

Homily, March 24, 2013

WHEN THE ALMOND TREE BLOOMS

—

Goodness always enchants us, truth fascinates us, life, happiness, and beauty attract us . . . Jesus is at the center of this mutual attraction, this duality. He is God and man: Jesus. God and man. But who takes the initiative? God, always! God's love always comes before our own! He always takes the initiative. He waits for us, He invites us in; the initiative is always His. Jesus is God made man, made flesh, He was born for us. The new star that appeared to the Magi was a sign of the birth of Christ. If they had not seen the star, those men would not have set out. Light precedes us, truth precedes us, beauty precedes us. God goes before us. The Prophet Isaiah said that God is like the flower of the almond tree. Why? Because in that region the almond tree is the first to bloom. And God always goes first; He always looks out for us; He always takes the first step.

Angelus, January 6, 2014

SAINT TERESA OF ÁVILA, TEACHER OF HAPPINESS

—

Teresa of Jesus asks her sisters to "go cheerfully" about their service (**The Way of Perfection** 18, 5). True holiness is a joy, because "a saint that is sad is a sad excuse for a saint." Saints, before being courageous heroes, are the fruit of God's grace to mankind. Every saint shows us a feature of the multifaceted face of God. In Saint Teresa we contemplate God, who, being the "sovereign Lord, of majesty supreme"

(**Poems** 2), reveals Himself as a close companion and experiences joy in conversing with humanity: God becomes joyful with us. And His love created a contagious joy in Saint Teresa, a joy that was impossible to hide, a radiant joy. This joy is a lifelong journey. It is neither instantaneous, superficial, nor tempestuous. One must look for it "even as a beginner" (**Life** 13, 1). Express the inner joy of the soul, for it is humble and "modest" (**The Book of Foundations** 12, 1). This joy is not reached by an easy shortcut, by skipping past sacrifice, suffering, or the Cross. No, it is found through suffering and sadness (**Life** 6, 2; 30, 8), looking to the Crucifix and seeking the Risen One (**The Way of Perfection** 26, 4). For this reason, Saint Teresa's joy is neither selfish nor self-referential. It is like the joy of Heaven, which is composed of "joy in the rejoicings of all" (**The Way of Perfection** 30, 5) and requires serving others with unselfish love. As she once instructed the nuns in her order, Saint Teresa would also tell us today, especially the young: "Always go about your day cheerfully!" (**Letter** 284, 4). The Gospel is not a lead sack that you drag around and that weighs you down, but a source of joy that fills the heart with God and impels us to serve our brothers!

Message, October 15, 2014

WHAT WILL MY PATH BE?

I, too, once asked myself: What path should I choose? But you do not have to choose a path—the Lord must choose it! Jesus will choose it! You only have to listen to Him and ask: Lord, what must I do?

This is the prayer that a young person should make: "Lord, what do you want from me?" With prayer and the advice of some good friends—your fellow lay people, priests, religious sisters, bishops, popes (even the Pope can offer good advice!)—you can find the path that the Lord wants for you.

Address, August 15, 2014

IN PRAISE OF REST

—

Rest is vital for our mental and physical health—yet it is often so difficult to obtain due to the many demands placed on us! Rest is also essential for our spiritual health, so that we can hear God's voice and understand what He asks of us.

Address, January 16, 2015

CULTIVATE YOUR FAITH BOTH IN MEN AND IN GOD

—

Often we trust a doctor, and this is good, because a doctor is meant to heal us. Sometimes we trust a person we know;

that is good, because our brothers and sisters can help us. It is good to trust one another. But we forget to trust in the Lord. This is the key to success in life. Trust in the Lord! Let's trust in the Lord! "Lord, look at my life: I'm lost, I'm struggling, I have sinned . . ." We can tell Him anything. "Look at what I have done: I trust in You!" This is a risk we have to take, to give ourselves to Him. He never disappoints. Never, ever! Listen carefully, you young people who are starting life now: Jesus never disappoints. Never. This is the testimony of John: Jesus, the Good One, the Meek One, who is like a lamb, will be slain. Without crying out. He came to save us, to take away sin. Mine, yours, the entire world's. All of our sin: all of it.

Homily, January 19, 2014

PRAY AND GIVE THANKS

—

The Apostle Saint Paul said to the Thessalonians: "Brothers, rejoice always." And how should we rejoice? He says: "Pray constantly, give thanks in every circumstance." Christian joy can be found in prayer, it comes from prayer and from giving thanks to God: "Thank you, Lord, for so many beautiful things!"

Homily, December 14, 2014

PREPARE A HOME FOR JESUS IN YOUR HEART

—

Joseph was chosen by God to be the foster father of Jesus and the husband of Mary. As Christians, you are called, like Joseph, to make a home for Jesus. To make a home for Jesus! You make a home for Him in your hearts, your families, your parishes, and your communities.

Address, January 16, 2015

THINK OF GOOD THINGS

Give thanks. How should I give thanks, you ask? Reflect on your life and think of the many good things that life has given you—so many! "But, Father, I have also received many bad things!" you say. "Yes, it's true, but that happens to all of us. Think of the good things," I say. "I was raised a Christian, I have Christian parents, thanks to God I have a job, my family does not suffer from hunger, we are all healthy . . ." The list goes on, there are so many things: Give thanks to the Lord for these. We get used to feeling joy from these things. Pray and give thanks . . .

Homily, December 14, 2014

The Secret of Life

The Beatitudes are the way
of life that the Lord teaches us,
so that we can follow in
His footsteps.
Homily, November 1, 2016

God keeps searching

As in the past, God searches for allies. He continues to search for men and women who are capable of belief, capable of creating history, capable of feeling part of His people enough to work with the creativity of the Holy Spirit. God travels through our neighborhoods and along our roads. He peers into every corner in search of hearts that are willing to listen to His invitation, to make His Word become flesh—here and now. Paraphrasing Saint Ambroeus, we could say that God continues to seek hearts that are similar to Mary's: willing to believe, even in the most extraordinary circumstances.

Homily, March 25, 2017

WE ARE NOT MADE FOR SMALL THINGS

—

Let us trust in God's work! With Him we can do great things; He can make us feel the joy of being His disciples, His witnesses. Take a chance on Christian ideals, on the most important things. We Christians were not chosen by the Lord for little things, so we should always go a little further, we should strive for the highest principles. Young people: Stake your lives on noble ideals!

Homily, April 28, 2013

CAN'T YOU FEEL HOW RESTLESS YOUR HEART IS?

—

The pursuit of happiness is common to people of every era and of every age. God has placed an irrepressible desire for happiness and fulfillment in the heart of every man and woman. Have you not noticed that your hearts are restless, always searching for something that can satisfy their thirst for the infinite?

Message for World Youth Day,
January 31, 2015

YOU WILL EXPERIENCE PEACE

—

In the Beatitudes, Jesus asks us to follow Him and to travel with Him along the path of love, the only path that leads to eternal life. It is not an easy road, but the Lord promises us His grace and never abandons us. Poverty, distress, humiliation, the struggle for justice, the hard work of conversion, the effort to remain faithful to our call to holiness, and persecutions—these are just some of the many challenges we face in our lives. But if we open the door to Jesus, if we bring Him into our lives, if we share our joys and sorrows with Him, then we will experience the peace and joy that only God, infinite love, can give.

Message for World Youth Day,
January 21, 2014

THE PATH TO TRUE
SELF-FULFILLMENT

—

It is always good for us to read and reflect on the Beatitudes! Jesus proclaimed them in His first great sermon, preaching from the shores of the Sea of Galilee. There was a very large crowd, and so Jesus went up on the mountain to teach His disciples. That is why it is known as "the Sermon on the Mount." In the Bible, the mountain is regarded as a place where God reveals Himself, and Jesus, by preaching on the mount, reveals Himself to be a divine teacher, a new Moses. And what does He tell us? He offers us a way of life, the way that He Himself has taken, the way that He **is:** He offers us **the path to true happiness**.

Message for World Youth Day,
January 21, 2014

Never let presumption blind you

—

God hides things from those who are full of themselves and who claim to know everything. They are blinded by their presumptuousness. They leave no room for God. Some of Jesus's contemporaries come to mind, people He repeatedly admonished, yet this danger still exists and concerns us, too. On the other hand, there are the "small" people: the humble, the simple, the poor, the marginalized, those without a voice, those who are weary and burdened. These are the people Jesus called "blessed." Mary, Joseph, the fishermen of Galilee, and the disciples, whom Jesus called out to as He went preaching, also come to mind.

Message, June 8, 2014

THE KINGDOM OF GOD IS IN THE BEATITUDES

—

Throughout His life, from His birth in the stable in Bethlehem to His death on the Cross and His Resurrection, Jesus embodied the Beatitudes. All the promises of God's Kingdom were fulfilled in Him.

Message for World Youth Day,
January 21, 2014

You Are Blessed Only When You Are Converted

—

Jesus manifests God's desire to lead men to happiness. This message was already present in the preaching of the prophets: God is close to the poor and the oppressed, and He delivers them from those who mistreat them. But in the Sermon on the Mount, Jesus follows a particular path: He starts with the word "blessed," which is to say, "happy." He continues with guidance on **how** to be happy; and He concludes by making a **promise**. The cause of blessedness, or happiness, lies not in your current state—for example, "the poor in spirit," "they who mourn," "they who hunger for righteousness," "the persecuted"—but in the subsequent promise Jesus makes, to be welcomed with faith as a gift from God. One starts from a condition of hardship so that one can open oneself to God's gift and enter the new world, the Kingdom announced by Jesus. This is not something that happens automatically: It is a way of life that comes from following the Lord. Thus the reality of hardship and affliction is seen from a new perspective and experienced according to the conversion that comes about. You are truly **blessed** only if you have **converted,** for only then are you able to appreciate and relish all of God's gifts.

Angelus, January 29, 2017

THE PURSUIT OF HAPPINESS

The word "blessed," meaning "happy," occurs nine times in Jesus's Sermon on the Mount, which is His first great sermon (Matthew 5:1–12). It is like a refrain reminding us of the Lord's call to advance together with Him on a road that, despite its many challenges, leads to true happiness.

Message for World Youth Day,
January 31, 2015

Mary's Magnificat introduces us to the Beatitudes

The **Magnificat** introduces us to the Beatitudes, the fundamental essence and Law of the Gospel message. In light of that, let us today ask for the wholly Christian grace that the future . . . be forged by the poor and the suffering, by the meek and those who hunger and thirst for righteousness, by the merciful and the pure in heart, by those who work in the name of peace and those who are persecuted for the sake of Christ's name, "for theirs is the Kingdom of Heaven" (Matthew 5:1–11).

May grace be forged by those who today are slaves in all but name, the ex-

ARE YOU A "THE MORE I HAVE, THE MORE I WANT" KIND OF PERSON?

—

"Blessed are the poor in spirit, for theirs is the Kingdom of Heaven" (Matthew 5:4). The poor in spirit are those who have adopted the feelings and attitudes of those who do not rebel, who know how to live humbly, meekly, and who are open to God's grace. The happiness of the poor—of the poor in spirit—is twofold: It encompasses both **riches** and **God.** With regard to possessions, to material possessions, their poverty in spirit manifests as sobriety. It is not a matter of sacrifice, but rather their ability to savor the essential, to share; their ability to begin each day anew, amazed by their bountiful goods, free from the muck of voracious consumerism. The more I have, the more I want, the more I have, the more I want: This is voracious consumerism. And it kills the soul. Men or women who do this, who have this "the more I have, the more I want" attitude, are not happy, and they will not find happiness, either. When it comes to God, happiness is found through praising Him, through recognizing that the world is a blessing and that it springs from the love of our Father, its Creator. Happiness is found by bowing before Him, by offering Him our meekness and docility: It is He, the Lord, He is the Great One. Not: I am great because I have so many things! It is He: He who wanted mankind to have the world, and He who wanted men and women to find happiness.

Angelus, January 29, 2017

MARY, POOR IN SPIRIT

—

We need to be converted so that the logic of **being more** will prevail over that of **having more**! To understand the profound meaning of the Beatitudes, we can turn to the saints . . .

The **Magnificat,** the Canticle of Mary, who was poor in spirit, is also the song of everyone who lives by the Beatitudes. The joy of the Gospel flows from a poor heart, a heart that knows how to rejoice and marvel at the works of God, a heart like the heart of Our Lady, whom all generations call "blessed" (Luke 1:48). May Mary, Mother of the poor and star of the new evangelization, help us to live the Gospel, to embody the Beatitudes in our lives, and have the courage to be happy.

Message for World Youth Day,
January 21, 2014

THE JOY OF POOR BELIEVERS

The most beautiful and spontaneous expressions of joy I have ever seen came from very poor people who have very few belongings. But I also remember the genuine joy of important professionals who were able to preserve a heart full of faith, generosity, and simplicity.

Evangelii Gaudium 7

BE A BEGGAR BEFORE GOD

As Saint Thérèse of the Child Jesus clearly saw, Jesus was incarnate among us as a beggar, a poor wanderer in search of our love. The **Catechism of the Catholic Church** tells us that man is a "beggar before God" (No. 2559) and that prayer is the encounter of God's thirst and our own thirst (No. 2560).

Saint Francis of Assisi perfectly understood the secret of the Beatitude of the poor in spirit. Indeed, when Jesus spoke to him through the leper and from the Crucifix, Francis recognized both God's grandeur and his own lowliness. In his prayer, the Poor Man of Assisi would spend hours asking the

Lord: "Who are you? Who am I?" He gave up a comfortable and carefree life in order to marry "Lady Poverty," to imitate Jesus and to follow the Gospel to the letter. Francis lived **in imitation of Christ in His poverty** and **in love for the poor.** For him the two were inextricably linked—like two sides of one coin.

Message for World Youth Day,
January 21, 2014

CHOOSE THE RICHNESS OF POVERTY, THE WEALTH OF THE POOR

So what is this poverty with which Christ frees us and enriches us? It is His way of loving us, His way of approaching us, just as the Good Samaritan approached the man left half dead by the side of the road (Luke 10:25). What gives us true freedom, true salvation, and true happiness is the compassion, tenderness, and solidarity of His love. The poverty of Christ enriches us, for He became flesh and He bears our weaknesses and sins as an expression of God's infinite mercy. Christ's poverty is the greatest treasure of all: Jesus's wealth is His boundless confidence in God the Father, His constant trust, His desire always and only to do the Father's will and give glory to Him. Jesus is rich in the same way as a child who feels loved and who loves her parents, a child who never doubts their love and tenderness. Jesus's wealth lies in being **the Son;** His unique relationship with the Father is the sovereign prerogative of this impoverished Messiah. When Jesus asks us to take up His "yoke, which is easy," He asks us to be enriched by His "poverty, which is rich" and by His "richness, which is poor," to share His filial and fraternal Spirit, to become sons and daughters in the Son, brothers and sisters to the firstborn Brother (Romans 8:29).

Léon Bloy said that the only real regret of life is not becoming a saint; we could also say that there is only one real kind of poverty: not living as children of God and brothers and sisters of Christ.

Message for Lent, 2014

DO YOU HAVE OPEN HANDS AND AN OPEN HEART?

—

The poor in spirit is the Christian who does not rely only on himself, on material wealth; who is not obstinate and opinionated, but who listens with respect; and who willingly defers to the decisions of others. If there were more of the poor in spirit in our communities, there would be fewer divisions, disagreements, and controversies! Humility, like charity, is an essential virtue for coexistence in Christian communities. The poor, in this evangelical sense, nurture the promise of the Kingdom of Heaven. They offer us a tiny glimpse of the Kingdom of Heaven, for a community that places sharing above ownership is as a seed to the Kingdom of Heaven. I would like to emphasize this: sharing over owning. The heart and hands must always be **open** [he gestures], not **closed** [he gestures]. When the heart is **closed** [he gestures], it is a shrunken heart. It doesn't even know how to love. When the heart is **open** [he gestures], it is on the path of love.

Angelus, January 29, 2017

THE CHURCH IS A HOME
FOR THE AFFLICTED

The Church, which is missionary in nature, is first and foremost charged with spreading charity to all. Universal fraternity and solidarity are innate to her life, to her mission in the world and for the world. We must evangelize, we must reach everyone, and we must begin with those who have the least, with the poor, with those who are weighed down by the burdens and strains of life. In so doing the Church prolongs the mission of Christ Himself, who "came so that they might have life and have it more abundantly" (John 10:10). The Church is for the common people of the Beatitudes, it is a home for the poor, the afflicted, the excluded, and the persecuted. It is home to those who hunger and thirst for righteousness.

Address, May 9, 2014

CULTIVATE THE GIFT
OF GENTLENESS

—

The gift of piety means being truly capable of rejoicing with those who rejoice, of weeping with those who weep, of staying close to those who are lonely or in anguish, of correcting those in error, of consoling the afflicted, of welcoming and helping those in need. The gift of piety is closely aligned with gentleness. The gift of piety is given to us by the Holy Spirit, and it makes us gentle, calm, and patient. This gift fills us with a God-given peace, and so we meekly, gently, seek to serve others.

General Audience, June 4, 2014

SEE THE FUTURE
WITH EYES OF FAITH

Let us look to the future with eyes of faith. Our pain is a seed that will one day bear fruit, because our Lord has promised joy to those who trust His words: "Blessed are they who mourn, for they will be comforted" (Matthew 5:4) . . . God's **compassion,** His suffering for us, gives eternal meaning and value to our struggles. The desire to thank Him for every grace and blessing, even if you have lost a great deal, is not only a triumph of resilience and strength ... it is also a sign of God's goodness, His closeness, His tenderness, and His salvation.

Homily, January 17, 2015

CHANGE THE WORLD, REDISCOVER HUMILITY

—

The Beatitudes are the image of Christ and, consequently, of each Christian. I would like to highlight one in particular: "Blessed are the meek." Jesus says of Himself: "Learn from Me, for I am meek and humble of heart" (Matthew 11:29). This is His spiritual likeness, and it reveals the abundance of His love. Meekness is a way of life, and living meekly brings us closer to Jesus and to one another. It allows us to set aside everything that divides us and thwarts us, and to find ever-new ways of advancing along the path of unity. The saints bring about change through their meekness of heart. With meekness, we understand God's greatness and we worship Him with full, sincere hearts. For meekness is the attitude of those who have nothing to lose—their only wealth is God.

Homily, November 1, 2016

THE WEAKNESS OF THE LAMB

Jesus is called "the Lamb": He is the Lamb who takes away the sin of the world. Someone might think: But how can a lamb, which is so weak, a weak little lamb, how can it take away so many sins, so much wickedness? With love. With His meekness. Jesus never ceased being a lamb: meek, good, full of love, close to the little ones, close to the poor. He was there, among the people, healing everyone, teaching, praying. Jesus was like a lamb, He was very weak. But He had the strength to take all our sins upon Himself, all of them. "But, Father, you don't know my life: I have such a sin [that is so great] I can't even carry it with a truck." Many times, when we examine our conscience, we find things there that are truly bad! But He carries them. He came for this: to forgive us, to bring peace to the world, but first to bring peace to our hearts. Perhaps each one of us feels troubled in his heart, perhaps he experiences darkness in his heart, perhaps he feels a little sad because of something he did wrong . . . He came to take away all of this, He gives us peace, He forgives everything. "Behold, the Lamb of God, who takes away sin": He takes away sin, root and all! This is the salvation that Jesus brings about by His love and His meekness. And in listening to what John the Baptist says, who bears witness to Jesus as the Savior, our confidence in Jesus can only grow.

Homily, January 19, 2014

GOSSIP,
THE ENEMY OF MEEKNESS
—

The virtue of meekness has fallen a little out of fashion these days. Being meek, giving up our place for others. There are many enemies of meekness, starting with gossip. Isn't that right? Sometimes we like to chitchat, we like to gossip about other people, and be a little spiteful. These are everyday situations, and they happen to everyone, even me.

But they are also temptations sent by the Evil One, who doesn't want the Spirit to come to us and bring us peace, who doesn't want our Christian communities to know meekness and mildness. We go to our church, and the ladies who do Sunday school are bickering with the ladies who do charity works. There are always these kinds of struggles. Even in our families, and in our neighborhoods. Even among friends! This is not being born again. When the Spirit comes to us and we are born again, we are meek, charitable. Now, don't judge anyone: The only judge is the Lord . . . If, with the grace of the Spirit, we managed not to gossip, it would be a giant step forward. And it would be good for everyone! Let us ask the Lord to show us and the rest of the world the beauty and greatness of this new life, this life born of the Spirit. Let us ask the Lord to help us be meek and charitable with one another—respectful of one another. Let us ask this grace for all of us.

Homily at Casa Santa Marta,
April 9, 2013

Don't be dazzled . . .

The light of Jesus is a humble light. It is not a bright light. It is humble. It is a mild light, a light with the strength of meekness. It is a light that speaks to the heart, and it is a light that offers the Cross. If we, in our inner light, can be meek and mild, we may hear the voice of Jesus in our hearts and look fearlessly at the Cross in the light of Jesus . . . But we must always make this distinction: Where Jesus is, there is always humility, meekness, love, and the Cross. We will never find Jesus without humility, meekness, love, and the Cross. He was the first to create this path of light. We must follow Him without fear, because Jesus has the strength and authority to give us this light.

Homily at Casa Santa Marta,
September 3, 2013

. . . IMITATE THE TRANQUIL LIGHT OF JESUS

—

Jesus's light is not a light of ignorance—no, not at all! It is a light of knowledge, of wisdom. But there is also another kind of light, the artificial light that the world offers us. It's bright, maybe even a little bit brighter than Jesus's? It's bright the way fireworks are bright, like the flash of a camera, whereas the light of Jesus is a mild light, a tranquil light, a light of peace. It's like the light of Christmas Eve: without pretense. It offers and gives peace. The light of Jesus doesn't make a big scene; it's a light that comes from the heart.

Homily at Casa Santa Marta,
September 3, 2013

CONTEMPLATE HIS SUFFERING

—

Only by contemplating the human suffering of Jesus can we become as meek, humble, and tender as He was. There is no other way. We need to truly study Jesus; we need to consider His passion and His suffering; we need to think about His meek silence. If we make this effort, He will take care of the rest. If anything is lacking, He will provide it. But you have to do this: Hide yourself, clothe yourself in God with Christ.

How do we bear witness? Contemplate Jesus.

How do we forgive? Contemplate how Jesus suffered.

How do we make sure not to hate our fellow man? Contemplate how Jesus suffered.

How do we make sure not to gossip about our fellow man? Contemplate how Jesus suffered.

There is no other way.

Homily at Casa Santa Marta,
September 3, 2013

You are a lamb, don't behave like a wolf

Jesus said to us: "I send you like a sheep amid wolves. Be careful, but simple." If we let ourselves be consumed by the spirit of vanity, if we hope to fight the wolves by becoming wolves ourselves, "they will eat you alive." Because if you stop being a sheep, you won't have a shepherd to defend you and you will fall into the hands of these wolves. You may ask yourselves: "Father, what weapon can we use to defend ourselves from the seductions, the fireworks that the prince of this world uses? How do we defend ourselves from his flattery?" The weapon is none other than Jesus: the Word of God, humility, and meekness. Think about Jesus when He was slapped: what humility and meekness He showed. He could have insulted them and instead He only asked a humble and meek question. Let us remember the passion of Christ. His prophet said of Him, "Like a sheep that goes to the slaughter, He didn't cry out." Humility. Humility and meekness: These are the weapons that the prince of the world, the spirit of the world cannot stand. His temptations are mundane, he tempts with vanity and wealth. Humility and meekness negate these temptations.

Homily at Casa Santa Marta, May 4, 2013

Go again and again and again

We feel shame to tell the truth: I did this, I thought that. But shame is a true Christian virtue. It is also very human! The capacity for shame ... I don't know if this is a saying in Italy, but in my country we call people who don't possess a sense of shame **sinvergüenza**. This means "without shame," because this person isn't capable of feeling shame. But shame is a virtue that comes from humility.

Humility and meekness are the mainstays of a Christian life. A Christian always strives for humility and meekness. And Jesus is waiting for us, ready to forgive us. We can ask Him any question: So, is going to Confession like going to a torture chamber? No! It is my chance to praise God because I am a sinner and I have been saved by Him. And is He waiting to beat me? No, He is waiting to forgive me with tenderness. And if I make the same mistake tomorrow? Then I will go again and again and again. He is always waiting for us. This is the Lord's tenderness, His humility, and His meekness.

Homily at Casa Santa Marta,
April 29, 2013

THEY'LL THINK YOU'RE STUPID

—

Jesus says: No war! No hate! Peace, meekness! Some people might object: "If I'm that meek in real life, everyone will think I am an idiot." Maybe so, but others will think that with your meekness you will inherit the earth!

Homily at Casa Santa Marta,
June 9, 2014

DON'T CONFUSE NOTHING WITH EVERYTHING

—

A Christian is meek, a Christian is magnanimous. He opens his heart wide. And when we find Christians with shriveled hearts, it means that they live with an egoism that masquerades as Christianity.

Jesus advised us: "First look for the Kingdom of God and His justice, and the rest will follow." The Kingdom of

God is everything; anything else comes second, is insignificant, nothing.

All the mistakes of the Church, all of our mistakes, are born of this first mistake: When we confuse anything with everything and when everything counts for nothing.

Homily at Casa Santa Marta,
June 17, 2013

FIGHT FOR JUSTICE
AND INJUSTICE

—

"Blessed are those who hunger and thirst for justice" is an affirmation addressed to those who struggle for justice, so that there can be justice in this world. Jesus says, "Blessed are those who fight against injustice." This is a doctrine that goes against the grain of what the world tells us.

Homily at Casa Santa Marta,
June 9, 2014

HUNGER FOR JUSTICE AND HUNGER FOR DIGNITY

—

You must give bread to the hungry—this is an act of justice. But there is also a deeper hunger, the hunger for a happiness that only God can satisfy: the hunger for dignity. Where there is ignorance of the fundamental pillars that govern a nation, there can be no real advancement of the common good, no real human development. The fundamental pillars are nonmaterial goods: **life,** which is a gift of God, a value always to be protected and promoted; the **family,** the foundation of harmony and a remedy against social fragmentation; **inner education,** which cannot be reduced to the transmission of information for gain or profit; **health,** which must encompass a person's entire well-being, including the spiritual dimension, which is essential for a balanced mind and a healthy existence; and **se-curity,** the conviction that violence can be overcome only by changing human hearts.

Homily, July 25, 2013

BE MERCIFUL SO THAT YOU, TOO, CAN BE FORGIVEN

—

Blessed are the merciful, because they will be shown mercy. We are talking about those who forgive, who understand other people's mistakes. Jesus does not say: Blessed are those who seek vengeance, who say an eye for an eye, a tooth for a tooth. He says: Blessed are those who forgive, those who are merciful. We are an army of the forgiven! All of us have been forgiven! And this is why he who takes the path of forgiveness is blessed.

Homily at Casa Santa Marta,
June 9, 2014

GOD IS JOYFUL BECAUSE HE IS MERCIFUL!

—

Chapter 15 of the Gospel of Luke contains three parables of mercy: the lost sheep, the lost coin, and then the longest of them—typical Saint Luke!—the parable of the father of two sons, the "prodigal" son and the son who believes he is "righteous" and saintly. All three of these parables speak of the joy of God. This is interesting: God is joyful! And what is the joy of God? The joy of God is mercy, the joy of God is forgiveness! It is the joy of a shepherd who finds his little lamb; it is the joy of a woman who finds her coin; it is the joy of a father welcoming home the son who was believed dead and who has come back to life, who has come home. Here is the entire Gospel! Here! The whole Gospel, all of Christianity, is right here! But take note: We are not talking about being politically correct, or about "do-goodery"! On the contrary, mercy is the true force that can save man and the world from the "cancer" that is sin—moral evil and spiritual evil. Only love fills the void, the empty abysses that evil opens up in hearts and in history. Only love can do this; and this, too, is God's joy!

Angelus, September 15, 2013

A PURE HEART IS A HEART THAT KNOWS HOW TO LOVE

—

"Blessed are the pure of heart" is one of Jesus's sayings that refers to those who have a fresh, clean, simple heart: a heart that knows how to love with a beautiful kind of purity.

Homily at Casa Santa Marta,
June 9, 2014

"Heart" means your ability to love

—

First of all, let us examine the biblical meaning of the word **heart**. In Hebrew thought, the heart is the center of man's emotions, thoughts, and intentions. Since the Bible teaches us that God does not look at appearances, but at the heart (1 Samuel 16:7), we can also say that it is with the heart that we see God. This is because the heart sums up the unity of body and soul, it defines a human being's ability to love and be loved in return.

Message for World Youth Day,
January 31, 2015

Don't miss out on the clarity life brings

—

As for the definition of the word **pure**, however, the Greek word used by the evangelist Matthew is **katharos**, which basically means "**clean**, **pure**, **undefiled** . . ."

Jesus responds categorically: "Nothing that enters one from outside can defile that person; but the things that come out from within are what defile . . . From within people, from their hearts, come evil thoughts, unchastity, theft, murder, adultery, greed, malice, deceit, licentiousness, envy, blasphemy, arrogance, folly" (Mark 7:15, 21–22).

How does happiness spring from a pure heart? From Jesus's list of the evils that make someone impure, we see that this question is ultimately about our **relationships** with other people.

Message for World Youth Day,
January 31, 2015

DEVELOP A HUMAN ECOLOGY

—

Each one of us must figure out what can "pollute" our heart. We must create an honest and precise conscience, so as to be capable to "discern what is the will of God, what is good and pleasing and perfect" (Romans 12:2). We need to show a healthy concern for taking care of creation, for the purity of our air, water, and food; but we need especially to protect the purity of what is most precious of all: **our heart and our relationships**. This "human ecology" will help us breathe the pure air that comes from inner beauty, from true love, and from holiness.

Message for World Youth Day,
January 31, 2015

PEACE DOES NOT MISUNDERSTAND OR DECEIVE

—

"Blessed are those who work for peace." It's very common to be a force for war, or at least a force for misunderstanding. An example of this is when I hear something from one person and then tell it to another person; and when I make my "second edition," it gets a little bigger in the telling. That's how gossip works, how people who gossip work; they do not work for peace. And they certainly aren't blessed.

Homily at Casa Santa Marta,
June 9, 2014

THERE'S NO FUTURE WITHOUT PEACE

—

Peace is not just the absence of war, but a general condition in which a person is in harmony with herself, with nature, and with other people. This is peace. Nevertheless, silencing weapons and extinguishing the hotbeds of war are absolutely necessary if we want to begin the journey toward peace, total peace. I'm thinking of the bloody infernos that still rage in too many parts of the world, of the tensions in families and in communities—for there is war in many families, in many communities, in parishes, too! There are heated disputes in our cities and towns between groups of different ethnic, cultural, and religious extraction. We must convince ourselves, despite every appearance to the contrary, that harmony is always possible, on every level and in every situation. There is no future without wishes and plans for peace! There is no future without peace!

Angelus, January 4, 2015

FIGHT FOR JUSTICE, DESPITE PERSECUTION

—

"Blessed are those who are persecuted for justice." How many people are persecuted—and have been persecuted— simply for fighting for justice!

Homily at Casa Santa Marta,
June 9, 2014

WE ARE SAVED AND THUS
WE ARE PERSECUTED

—

God has redeemed us. He chose us out of His pure grace. His death and Resurrection released us from the power of the world, the power of the Devil, from the power of the prince of this world. This is the origin of all hatred: We are saved and the prince of the world doesn't want us to be saved and so he hates us. He has encouraged our persecution from the days of Jesus right through today. Many Christian communities throughout the world are persecuted. And more now than in the early times: How about that! Now, here, today, right now. Why? Because the prince of the world hates us.

Homily at Casa Santa Marta,
May 4, 2013

MAKE STRONG AND RADICAL CHOICES

—

Trusting in the faith of the Lord is a choice that we can make in our Christian lives ... It's a great and difficult decision. We realize this when we read about the life of martyrs and when we read the news about the persecution of Christians today. Let us think of our brothers and sisters who find themselves in extreme situations and who choose to trust in the Lord. They live in our times. They are an example to us. They encourage us to offer the Church our whole livelihood.

Homily at Casa Santa Marta,
November 25, 2013

START A HAPPINESS REVOLUTION; GO AGAINST PREVAILING THOUGHT

The Beatitudes of Jesus are a new and revolutionary model of happiness that contradicts what is usually communicated by the media and prevailing wisdom. A worldly way of thinking finds it scandalous that God became one of us and died on a cross! According to this worldly logic, those whom Jesus proclaimed blessed are regarded as useless, as "losers." On the other hand, success at any cost is glorified, as are creature comforts, the arrogance of power, and self-absorption.

Message for World Youth Day,
January 21, 2014

Your identity card as a Christian

—

The Beatitudes are in some sense a Christian's **identity card**. They identify us as followers of Jesus. We are called on to be blessed, to be followers of Jesus, to confront the troubles and anxieties of our age with the spirit and love of Jesus. Thus we ought to be able to recognize and respond to new situations with fresh spiritual energy. Blessed are those who remain faithful while enduring evils inflicted on them by others, and who forgive them from their heart. Blessed are those who look into the eyes of the abandoned and marginalized and show them compassion. Blessed are those who see God in every person, and who strive to help others discover Him. Blessed are those who protect and care for our common home. Blessed are those who renounce their own well-being for the good of others. Blessed are those who pray and work for full communion among Christians. They are all messengers of God's mercy and tenderness, and surely they will receive from Him their deserved reward.

Homily, November 1, 2016

Free and Liberated People

Take great care of your spiritual
life, for it is the source of inner
freedom. Without prayer, inner
freedom does not exist.
ADDRESS, JUNE 6, 2013

FREE YOURSELF FROM THE POWER OF THINGS

—

First of all, try to be **free with regard
to material things**. The Lord calls us
to a Gospel lifestyle marked by sobriety.
We should not give in to consumerism.
This means focusing on the essentials
and learning to do without all those
extra, useless things that suffocate us.
Let us distance ourselves from the longing to possess things, from the idolatry
of money, and from wastefulness.

Let's put Jesus first. He can free us from the kinds of idol worship that enslave us. Put your trust in God! He knows us, He loves us, and He never forgets us. Just as He provides for the lilies of the field (Matthew 6:28), so He will make sure that we lack nothing.

If we are to overcome the financial crisis, we must be ready to change our lifestyle and avoid such overindulgence. Just as we need the courage to be happy, we also need the courage to live simply.

Message for World Youth Day,
January 21, 2014

GO BEYOND CALCULATING THE PRODUCTIVITY OF YOUR MISSION

Finally, it is important to let the Gospel teach us the way of proclamation. At times, despite our best intentions, we can indulge in a certain hunger for power, proselytism, or intolerant fanaticism. Yet the Gospel tells us to reject the idolatry of power and success, to stop worrying about social hierarchies, and to reject the kind of anxiety that has more to do with the spirit of conquest than that of service. The seed of the Kingdom, however tiny, however invisible or insignificant, is always growing, thanks to God's tireless activity. "The Kingdom of God . . . is as if a man were to scatter seed on the land and would sleep and rise night and day and the seed would sprout and grow, he knows not how" (Mark 4:26–27). This is our first reason for confidence: God surpasses all our expectations and constantly surprises us by His generosity. He makes our efforts bear fruit beyond all calculations of productivity.

Message for World Day of Prayer for Vocations, 2017

Stop sitting at the table of slavery

—

In our existential journey there is a tendency to resist liberation; we are afraid of freedom and, paradoxically, we unconsciously prefer slavery. Freedom frightens us because it asks us to confront time and to face our responsibility to live it well. Slavery, on the other hand, reduces time to a single moment: It severs each moment from both the past and the future, and that makes us feel safer. In other words, slavery prevents us from truly and fully living in the present, because it makes our past empty and cuts off our future, separates us from eternity. Slavery makes us believe that we cannot dream, fly, hope.

A great Italian artist once said that it was easier for the Lord to take the Israelites out of Egypt than to take Egypt out of the heart of the Israelites. Yes, the Israelites were physically freed from slavery, but while wandering in the desert, faced with many difficulties and their hunger, they began to feel nostalgia for Egypt, and they remembered when they ate "the onions, and the garlic" (Numbers 11:5). They forgot, however, that they ate them at the table of slavery. Nostalgia for slavery is nestled in our hearts because it is seemingly more reassuring than freedom, which is far riskier. How we like being captivated by lots of fireworks, which are beautiful at first glance but which in reality last a few seconds! This is the power, the charm of the moment!

Homily, December 31, 2014

BE HUMANE BECAUSE YOU ARE MORE THAN HUMAN

—

We become truly humane when we are more than human, when we let God lead us beyond ourselves to reach our truest essence. This is the source and inspiration of all our efforts at evangelization. For if we have received a love that restores all meaning to our lives, how can we fail to share that love with others?

Evangelii Gaudium 8

FREE YOURSELF SO THAT YOU CAN GIVE YOURSELF

—

The Lord gives us true freedom. First, there is freedom from sin, from selfishness in all its forms: the freedom to give oneself and to do it with joy, like the Virgin of Nazareth. She is free of self-love, She does not complain about Her condition—although She would have had reason to!—but She thinks of people who are in greater need. Her freedom is the freedom of God, which is manifested as love. And this is the freedom that God has given to us, and we must not lose it: the freedom to adore

God, to serve God, and to serve Him also in our brothers.

Homily, July 5, 2014

DON'T BE A SLAVE TO YOUR AMBITIONS

What does having inner freedom mean?

First of all, it means being free from personal goals and projects . . . Freedom from programming your future . . . It means, in a certain way, freeing yourself from your culture and its mindset. This is not about forgetting or denying where you come from, but rather opening yourselves up, warmly, charitably, to cultures and people very distant and very different from your own. Above all it means being alert and steering clear of the ambitions or personal aims that can cause the Church great harm. You must be careful not to make either your own fulfillment or the recognition you might receive both inside and outside the ecclesiastical community a constant priority. Rather, your priority should be the loftier good of the Gospel cause and the accomplishment of the mission entrusted to you. I think being free from ambitions or personal goals is important, very important. Careerism is a form of leprosy. Leprosy! No careerism, please.

Address, June 6, 2013

GOD WANTS WOMEN AND MEN WITHOUT CHAINS

—

God shows us that He is the good Father. How does He do this? He does it through the incarnation of His Son, who became one of us. Through this man called Jesus we can understand what God truly intends. He wants human beings to be free so they can always feel protected, like children of a good father.

To fulfill this design, God needs only

one human being. He needs one woman, a mother, to place the Son in the world. She is the Virgin Mary, whom we honor with [this evening's] Vespers. Mary was completely free. She freely said yes. And so She has done us all an eternal good. In this way She served God and mankind—God **and** mankind! Let us imitate Her example if we want to know what God expects from us, His children.

Meeting, August 5, 2014

Always reflect
on your actions

—

I would like to discuss two fundamental values: freedom and service. First of all: Be free people! What do I mean by that? Some people might think that freedom means doing whatever you want, seeing how far you can go, seeking thrills to overcome boredom . . . This is not freedom. Freedom means being able to think about what we do, being able to judge what is good and what is bad. Freedom means always choosing the good, because this type of behavior leads to growth. Let us be free in order to be good. Do not be afraid to go against the flow, even if it is not easy! Being free to choose goodness is demanding but it will make you into a person with backbone, someone who can face life and people with courage and patience (**parrhesia** and **ypomonē**).

Address, June 7, 2013

ANXIETY IS A GOOD SEED

When I hear that a young man or woman feels anxious, I feel it is my duty to take care of them and to listen to their anxiety. Anxiety is like a seed, because it, too, will grow and create fruit. Right now I feel that I am doing you a service by tending to the most precious thing in this moment for you, which is your anxiety.

Meeting with Young People,
March 31, 2014

EMBRACE THE COMMANDMENTS AS A PATH TO SELF-FULFILLMENT

—

The Ten Commandments show us the path to freedom, a guide carved not on stone tablets but on the heart (2 Corinthians 3:3). The Ten Commandments are here, inscribed on our hearts! We can see this most clearly when God gave the Ten Commandments to the People of Israel through Moses. At the Red Sea the people experienced great liberation; they had tangible proof of the power and faithfulness of God, the God who set them free. Then, on Mount Sinai, God Himself gives His people, and all of us, the path to freedom, a path that is engraved in the human heart as a universal moral law (Exodus 20:1–17; Deuteronomy 5:1–22). We must not see the Ten Commandments as limiting our freedom—no, that is not what they do—but rather as signposts **to** our freedom. They are not restrictions, they are guiding lights! They teach us to avoid the slavery we condemn ourselves to, to avoid the many false idols that we ourselves build—we have seen this in history, and we still see it today. They teach us to open ourselves to a more generous existence, one that is not materialistic. They teach us to show people respect, to overcome our greed for power, for possessions, and for money, to be honest and sincere in our relationships. They teach us to protect the whole of creation and to nourish our planet with lofty, noble spiritual ideals. Following the Ten Commandments means being faithful to ourselves and to our most authentic nature. It is a path that leads toward the genuine freedom that Christ taught us in the Beatitudes.

Videomessage, June 8, 2013

ENTER INTO THE
TRINITARIAN LIFE
—

"Yes, Father, such has been your gracious will" (Luke 10:21). These words of Jesus refer to **His inner exultation** where the word "gracious" describes the Father's saving and benevolent plan for humanity. Divine graciousness made Jesus rejoice because the Father decided to love humanity with the same love that He has for His Son. Luke speaks of a similar exultation in Mary: "My soul proclaims the greatness of the Lord, my spirit rejoices in God my Savior" (Luke 1:46–47). This is the Good News that leads to salvation. Mary carried Jesus, the evangelizer par excellence, in Her womb when She went to Elizabeth and rejoiced in the Holy Spirit as She sang Her **Magnificat**. In Jesus's case, when He saw the success of His disciples' mission and their resulting joy, He rejoiced in the Holy Spirit and addressed His Father in prayer. In both cases, the working of salvation brings deep joy: The love that the Father feels for His Son reaches us, the Holy Spirit fills us, and we enter into the Trinitarian life.

Message, June 8, 2014

IT IS GOD WHO SETS US FREE

—

The Living God sets us free! So let us say yes to love and no to selfishness. Let us say yes to life and no to death. Let us say yes to freedom and no to being a slave to the many idols of our time. In a word, let us say yes to the God who is love, life, and freedom and who never disappoints (1 John 4:8, 11:2, 8:32); let us say yes to the God who is the Living One and the Merciful One. Only faith in the Living God saves us: in the God who in Jesus Christ has given us His own life; who in the gift of the Holy Spirit has made it possible to live as true sons and daughters of God through His mercy. This faith brings us freedom and happiness.

Homily, June 16, 2013

THOSE WHO FOLLOW THE COMMANDMENTS SAY YES TO LOVE

—

True freedom is not about following our egos, our blind passions; it is about love, about choosing the good in every situation. The Ten Commandments are not a hymn to "no," they are a hymn to "yes." A yes to God, a yes to Love, and since I say yes to Love, I say no to non-Love . . . but the no is a consequence of that yes that comes from God and which makes us love!

Let us rediscover and live out the Ten Words of God! Let us say yes to these "ten paths of love," which were perfected by Christ to defend and guide human beings to true freedom!

Videomessage, June 8, 2013

READ THE SIGNS OF GOD IN YOUR LIFE

—

Always love Jesus Christ more and more! Our life is a response to His call. You will be happy and will build a good life if you answer this call. Feel the Lord's presence in your life. He is close to each one of you as a companion; He is a friend who knows how to help and understand you, who encourages you in difficult times, and who never abandons you. In prayer, in conversation with Him, and in reading the Bible, you will discover that He is close by. You will also learn to read the signs of God in your life. He always speaks to us, even through the events of our time and our daily life; it is up to us to listen to Him.

Address, June 7, 2013

PART II

YOU AND OTHERS: HAPPINESS IN YOUR RELATIONSHIPS

Let Your Light Be Contagious

Receiving and bringing
God's consolation: This is an
urgent mission.
HOMILY, OCTOBER 1, 2016

THE SECRET TO A GOOD LIFE

The secret to a good life is to love and to surrender to love. By doing this, we find the strength to "sacrifice ourselves with joy," and so the most difficult task becomes a source of great joy. By doing this, we are no longer afraid to make important choices in life. Instead, their true colors are revealed: Our choices are a way for us to attain self-fulfillment and personal freedom.

Address, April 21, 2014

SERVING OTHERS FREES US FROM SADNESS, FROM "WHAT GETS US DOWN"

We experience freedom when, with the grace of God, we put ourselves at the service of others, when we serve our Christian communities. Without jealousy, without bias, without gossip: That is serving one another! When we do this, the Lord frees us from the ambition and rivalry that undermine the unity of communion. He frees us from distrust and sadness—sadness is especially dangerous because it gets us down. Sadness brings us down, it's dangerous, so be careful! He frees us from fear, from inner emptiness, isolation, regret, and complaints. Even in our communities, there are still negative attitudes that make people self-centered, more concerned with defending themselves than with giving themselves.

But Christ frees us from this existential grayness, as we proclaimed in the Responsorial Psalm, "You are my help and my liberation." Even though we are weak and sinners—we all are!—we are the disciples of the Lord and we are called on to live our faith with joy and courage, in communion with God and with our brothers, and in adoration of God. We are called on to face life's labors and trials with fortitude.

Homily, July 5, 2014

BRING PEACE, BRING THE BALM OF JESUS

We are anointed. The word "Christian" means "the anointed ones." And why are we anointed? To do what? "He sent me to bring the Good News"—to whom? "To the afflicted, to bind up the brokenhearted, to proclaim liberty to the captives, and release to the prisoners; to announce a year of favor from the Lord" (Isaiah 61:1–2). This is the vocation of Christ and the vocation of all Christians. To help others in need, whether their needs be material or spiritual . . . Many people suffer anxiety because of family problems . . . Bring them peace, too, bring the balm of Jesus, the oil of Jesus, which does so much good and soothes the soul.

Homily, December 14, 2014

HAPPINESS CAN'T BE BOUGHT
—

None of us knows what life may bring. You young people wonder, "What is in store for me?" We can do bad things, even very bad things, but please, do not despair: The Father is always waiting for us! Come back, He says! Come back! These are His words: Come back! Come home, because your Father is waiting for you. And if I am a great sinner, He will celebrate me all the more. And to the priests: Embrace your sinners and please be merciful. Mercy is a beautiful feeling. It brings me great happiness to know that God never tires of forgiving. He never tires of waiting for us to come home.

Address, August 15, 2014

THE CONTAGIOUSNESS OF JOY: THIS IS HOW THE GOSPEL IS SPREAD

—

When Jesus sent the Twelve out on a mission, He said to them: "Do not take gold or silver or copper for your belts; no sack for the journey, or a second tunic, or sandals, or walking stick. The laborer deserves his keep" (Matthew 10:9–10). Evangelical poverty is the fundamental condition for spreading the Kingdom of God. The most beautiful and spontaneous expressions of joy I have ever seen were those of poor people who had few worldly goods. Evangelization in our time will only take place as the result of contagious joy.

Message for World Youth Day,
January 21, 2014

LEARN, AND TEACH OTHERS, TO DISCERN

When we are children, it's easy for Mom and Dad to tell us what to do . . . I'm not sure it happens much anymore, but back in my day it did. Today I am not so sure, but still it was much easier then! As we grow up, we find ourselves surrounded by many voices, all of whom seem to be right. This is when discernment becomes crucial, for it leads to life and resurrection—to life, and not to a culture of death. I talk about this a great deal because it is important. Discernment is important for catechism and for life. Discernment needs to be part of catechism, spiritual guidance, and homilies; we need to teach children, young people, and adults to discern! We need to teach them to ask for the grace of discernment.

Address, March 25, 2017

CHRIST IS KNOCKING AT THE DOOR OF YOUR HEART. KNOCK ON THE DOORS OF YOUR BROTHERS' HEARTS

Today Christ is knocking at the door of your heart . . . and my heart, too! He asks us to rise up, to be awake and alert, and to see only what really matters in life. What is more, He asks you and me to go out on the streets and roads of this world and knock on the doors of other people's hearts, inviting them to welcome Him into their lives.

Address, August 15, 2014

He who loves the poor brings the Gospel, not communism

—

I am a believer. I believe in God, I believe in Jesus Christ, and I believe in the Gospel. The heart of the Gospel is in the message to the poor. When you read the Beatitudes, for example, or Matthew 25, you will see how clear Jesus is about this. This is the heart of the Gospel. Jesus said of Himself, "I came to deliver the message of liberation, of health, and of God's grace to the poor . . ." To the poor! To those who need salvation, who need to be welcomed into society. Then, if you read the Gospel, you will see that Jesus had a certain preference for the marginalized: lepers, widows, orphans, the blind . . . all marginalized people. Even great sinners . . . and this comforts me! Yes, because He is not afraid of sin! When He found someone like Zacchaeus, a thief, or Matthew, who betrayed his country for money,* He wasn't afraid! He saw them and He chose them. The poverty of sin is also a kind of poverty. For me, the poor are at the heart of the Gospel. Two months ago, I heard someone say, "This Pope is a communist." No! This is the mark, the token of the Gospel, not of communism! It's the Gospel that speaks of poverty without ideology, only poverty . . . This is why I think that the poor are at the center of Jesus's message.

Meeting with Young People,
March 31, 2014

---

*As tax collectors working for the Roman Empire, Matthew and Zacchaeus may have been perceived as thieves and traitors by other Jews.

REACH OUT TO OTHERS AND
SEEK THEIR WELL-BEING
—

Goodness tends to spread. Every authentic experience of truth and goodness seeks by its very nature to grow within us, and any person who has experienced that profound liberation becomes more sensitive to the needs of others. As it expands, goodness takes root and develops. To lead a dignified and fulfilling life, we need to reach out to others and seek their well-being.

Evangelii Gaudium 9

TRUE JOY COMES
FROM AN ENCOUNTER
—

Worldly things may satisfy some desires and give us certain emotions, but ultimately those are shallow pleasures, superficial joys. They are not intimate joys. They offer us momentary tipsiness that does not make us really happy.

True joy is not a momentary tipsiness: It is something else altogether!

Real joy does not come from possessing material things—no! It is born from the encounter, from a relationship with others. It is born from feeling accepted, understood, and loved; and it is born from accepting, understanding, and loving others . . . not because of a passing fancy but because the other is a person, too. Joy is born from the graciousness of an encounter! It comes from hearing someone say, not necessarily with words: "You are important to me." This is beautiful . . . And it is these very words that God uses to make us understand, too. In calling out to you, God says, "You are important to Me, I love you, I am counting on you." Jesus says this to each one of us! Joy is born from that! That is the joy of an encounter with Jesus. Understanding and hearing this is the secret of our joy. Feeling loved by God, feeling that we are not just numbers to Him but individual souls; feeling that it is He who is calling us. Becoming a priest or a religious man or woman is not really our decision. I do not believe that seminarian or that novice who says: "I have chosen this path." I don't think so! It doesn't work like that! Rather, it is the response to a call, to a call of love. I feel something within me, something stirring and moving, and I answer "Yes." It is in prayer that the Lord makes us feel His love, but also through many signs that we can read in our lives, in the many people He sets on our path. And the joy of the encounter with Him and of hearing His call does not lead to shutting oneself in, but to opening oneself up; it leads to service in the Church.

Meeting with Seminarians and Novices,
July 6, 2013

DRY YOUR TEARS AND THOSE OF YOUR BROTHERS AND SISTERS

—

"Comfort, give comfort to my people" (Isaiah 40:1) are the words of the prophet that still bring hope to those who experience suffering and pain. Let us never allow ourselves to be robbed of the hope born of faith in the Risen Lord. True, we are often sorely tested, but we must never lose our certainty of the Lord's love for us. His mercy is also expressed in the closeness, affection, and support that many of our brothers and sisters offer us in times of sadness and suffering. We often find ourselves trapped in a vicious cycle of solitude, but the drying of tears can break this cycle.

Misericordia et Misera 13

GO TO THE POOR,
DON'T JUST TALK ABOUT IT

—

All of us need to experience a conversion when it comes to how we see the poor. We have to care for them and be sensitive to their spiritual and material needs. To you, to the youth of today, I especially entrust the task of bringing solidarity with the poor back to the center of human culture. Faced with old and new forms of poverty—unemployment, migration, addictions of various kinds—it is our duty to be alert and thoughtful, to avoid the temptation of indifference. We have to remember all those who feel unloved, who have no hope for the future, and who have given up on life out of discouragement, disappointment, or fear. We have to learn to stand with the poor, to be on their side, and not just indulge in pretty language! Let us go out to meet them, look into their eyes, and listen to them. The poor provide us with a concrete opportunity to encounter Christ Himself, and to touch His suffering flesh.

Message for World Youth Day,
January 21, 2014

WHAT REMAINS AT THE END?
GOD AND OUR FELLOW MAN!

In today's Gospel, God asks us about the meaning of life. Using an image, we could say that these readings serve as a "sieve" through which our life can be poured: They remind us that almost everything in this world will pass away, like running water. But the real treasures remain, like jewels caught in a sieve. So what stays, what adds meaning to life, what riches never vanish? For sure, there are two: **the Lord** and **our neighbor**. These two riches do not disappear! These are the greatest goods, the most cherished. Everything else—the heavens, the earth, all that is most beautiful, even the Basilica of Saint Peter—will pass away; so we must always include **God** and **other people** in our lives.

Homily, November 13, 2016

WHAT DO YOU TREASURE?

What do you treasure? What does your heart hold dear? Our hearts can be attached to true or false treasures; they can find genuine rest or they can doze off and become lazy and lethargic. The most precious thing we have in life is our relationship with God. Do you believe this? Do you realize how much you are worth in the eyes of God? Do you know that you are loved and welcomed by Him unconditionally, as you are?

When we lose sight of this, we human beings become a puzzle with no answer, because it is the knowledge that God loves us unconditionally that gives our lives meaning. Do you remember the conversation that Jesus had with the rich young man (Mark 10:17–22)? Mark the Evangelist observes that the Lord looked upon him and loved him (verse 21) and invited him to follow Him and thus to find true riches.

Message for World Youth Day,
January 31, 2015

WHERE DOES YOUR HEART LIE?

—

I want to ask you a question. It is not an original one, it comes from the Gospel. But I think, after listening to you, that it is perhaps the right question at this time for you. What do you treasure? This is the question. Where does your heart lie? What does your heart hold dear? Because where your treasure lies, your life lies, too. Each of our hearts is attached to a treasure, something that all of us hold close. Is it power, money, pride . . . ? Or is it kindness, generosity, the desire to do good things . . . ? There are many kinds of treasure . . . What will be yours? This is the question that I ask you, but you have to answer it yourselves, on your own, at home . . .

Meeting with Young People,
March 31, 2014

WHAT KIND OF MAN OR WOMAN DO YOU WANT TO BECOME: SELFISH, OR FRATERNAL?

—

True fraternal love wins out over individual selfishness, because selfishness prevents us from living in freedom and harmony. Such selfishness develops socially—through corruption, which is so widespread today, or through the formation of criminal organizations, from small gangs to ones organized on a global scale. These groups undermine legality and justice and strike at the very heart of human dignity.

These organizations gravely offend God, they harm our brothers, and they harm creation—all the more so if they have religious overtones.

I think of the heartbreaking drug abuse crisis, which profits in defiance of all moral and civil laws. I think of the devastation of natural resources, of the constant pollution, and the tragedy of the exploitation of labor. I think of illicit money trafficking and financial speculation, which often prey on and cripple entire economies and nations, exposing millions of men and women to poverty. I think of prostitution, which every day claims fresh victims, especially the young, robbing them of their future. I think of the abomination of human trafficking, the crimes and abuses against minors, the horror of slavery still present in many parts of the world; of the frequently overlooked tragedy of migrants, who are often victims of disgraceful and illegal manipulation.

Message for World Day of Peace, 2014

LEARN FROM THE WISDOM OF THE POOR

—

The poor are not just people we give to: They have **much to offer and teach us.** We have much to learn from the wisdom of the poor! Think of the eighteenth-century saint Benedict Joseph Labre, who slept on the streets of Rome and lived off the alms he received, yet became a spiritual guide to all sorts of people, including nobles and prelates. In a way, the poor are our teachers. They show us that a person's worth is not measured by their possessions or how much money they have in their bank account. A poor person, a person lacking material possessions, always preserves his or her dignity. The poor can also teach us much about humility and trust in God. In the parable of the Pharisee and the tax collector (Luke 18:9–14), Jesus holds the tax collector up as a model because of his humility and his acknowledgment that he is a sinner. The widow who gave her last two coins to the Temple treasury is an example of the generosity of all those who have next to nothing and yet give away everything they have (Luke 21:1–4).

Message for World Youth Day,
January 21, 2014

LET THE CHURCH BE THE SOURCE OF YOUR CONSOLATION

God does not comfort us only in our hearts; through the prophet Isaiah He adds, "In Jerusalem you shall find your comfort" (66:13). In Jerusalem—that is, in the city of God, in the community. When we are united in communion, God's consolation works in us.

In the Church we find consolation. It is **the house of consolation:** here God wishes to console us. We may ask ourselves: As a member of the Church, do I bring the consolation of God to others? Do I know how to welcome others as guests and console those whom I see as tired and disillusioned? Even when suffering from affliction and rejection, a Christian is called upon to bring hope to the hearts of those who have given up, to encourage the downhearted, to bring the light of Jesus, the warmth of His presence, and His restorative forgiveness. Many people suffer; many people endure hardship and injustice; many people live in anxiety. Our hearts need anointing with God's consolation, which does not take away our problems but gives us the power to love, and to peacefully bear pain.

Homily, October 1, 2016

THE PATH TO GOD IS THROUGH DIALOGUE

Q. (**Girl**): I see God in others. Where do you see God?

A. (**Pope Francis**): I am constantly looking for Him! I look for Him in all walks of life. I look . . . and I find Him when I read the Bible, I find Him in the celebration of the Sacraments, in prayer. I try to find Him in my work, in other people, all kinds of people . . . I find Him above all in the sick: Being with sick people is good for me, because when I am with a sick person, I ask myself: Why is he ill and I am not? And I find Him also when I am with prisoners: Why is he in prison and I am not? I talk to God. I say, "You're always so unfair: Why him and not me?" I find God through this. I always find Him in dialogue. It's good for me to look for God throughout the day. I don't always manage to, but I try to always be in dialogue. The saints were good at this; I have to get better at it. But this is the path.

Meeting with Young People,
March 31, 2014

WE ALL NEED CONSOLATION

All of us need consolation. No one is immune to suffering, pain, and misunderstanding. How much pain can be caused by a spiteful remark; and the remark itself is the result of envy, jealousy, or anger! What great suffering is caused by betrayal, violence, and abandonment! What bitterness we feel when faced with the death of a loved one! Yet God is never far away, even at these traumatic moments. An encouraging word; a hug that makes us feel understood, makes us feel loved; a prayer that gives us strength . . . these are all expressions of the closeness of

God, which He offers us through the consolation of our brothers and sisters.

Misericordia et Misera 13

WE ARE REFLECTIONS OF HIS TRANSFORMING LIGHT

—

Jesus invites us to be a reflection of His light through the testimony of good works. He says: "Your light must shine before others, that they may see your good deeds and glorify your Heavenly Father" (Matthew 5:16). These words emphasize that we are recognized as true disciples of Him who is the Light of the World, not through our words, but through our works. Indeed, it is above all our behavior that—good or bad—leaves a mark on others. Therefore, we have a duty and a responsibility to the gift we receive: We must not hold back the light of the faith—which is in us through Christ and the Holy

Spirit—as if it were ours alone, our property. Instead we are called to make it shine throughout the world, to offer it to others through good works. How much the world needs the light of the Gospel: a light that transforms, heals, and guarantees salvation to those who receive it! We must convey this light through our good works.

Angelus, February 5, 2017

A SMILE CAN CHANGE YOUR LIFE

Let us ask ourselves—as both individuals and communities—how do we react when we come across people in our daily lives who might be victims of human trafficking? How do we react when we are tempted to buy products that may have been made by exploiting others? Some of us—out of indifference, or because we are distracted by daily concerns, or for financial reasons—turn a blind eye. But other people decide to take action: They join civic associations or practice small, everyday gestures—and these gestures have real merit!—like saying a kind word, a greeting, a "Good morning!" or even a smile. These gestures cost us nothing but they can offer hope, open doors, and change the life of someone stuck in the shadows. These invisible people can change our lives, too, when it comes to this kind of thing.

Message for World Day of Peace, 2015

YOUR COMPASSION CAN BE OFFERED IN SILENCE

—

Sometimes **silence** can be a great help; because sometimes there are no words, no answers for the questions of those who suffer. But in the absence of words, silence can be seen in the compassion of a person who stays by our side, who loves us and who holds out a hand to us. It is not true that silence is a kind of surrender. On the contrary, it is a show of strength and love. Silence is part of our language of consolation; it is a concrete way to share in the suffering of a brother or sister.

Misericordia et Misera 13

A COMMUNION OF LOVE
—

It is not enough to know that God is born; we must celebrate **Christmas in our hearts**. God is born, yes, but is He born in your heart? Is He born in my heart? Is He born in our hearts? In this way we will find Him with Mary and Joseph in the stable, as the Magi did.

The Magi went forth. When they found the Child, "they prostrated themselves and did Him homage" (Matthew 2:11). They did not just look at Him, they did not just say a circumstantial prayer and leave. No! **They worshipped Him:** They entered into a personal communion of love with Jesus.

Angelus, January 6, 2017

WE ARE THE SALT THAT GIVES FLAVOR

—

When we give, the light of our faith does not fade. It gets stronger. However, it can weaken if we do not nourish it with love and charitable works . . .

The mission of Christians in society is to give "flavor" to life using the faith and the love that Christ has given us. At the same time, we must guard against the contaminating germs of selfishness, envy, slander, and so on.

Each one of us is called to be both **light** and **salt** in our daily lives, persevering in the task of restoring the spirit of the Gospel and the vision of the Kingdom of God to humanity.

Angelus, February 5, 2017

ADDING WATER TO THE BEANS

—

It is important to know how to welcome people. It is more beautiful than any kind of ornament or decoration. I say this because when we are generous in welcoming people and sharing something with them—a bit of food, a place in our homes, our time—we are not poorer for it: We are enriched. I know that when someone in need of food knocks on your door, you always find a way of sharing food with them. As the proverb says, one can always "add more water to the beans!" Can you add more water to the beans? . . . Always? What is more, you can do it with love, demonstrating that true riches are found not in material things, but in the heart!

Address, July 25, 2013

KINDNESS IS MORE REWARDING THAN MONEY

Differences do not stand in the way of harmony, joy, and peace; rather, they are opportunities for deeper mutual knowledge and understanding. Being open to a wide variety of religious experiences shows true and reverential love for one's neighbor; every religious community expresses itself through love and not violence, and is never ashamed of showing kindness! People who nourish kindness in their heart find that such kindness leads to a peaceful conscience and to profound joy even in the midst of difficulties and misunderstandings. Even when affronted, kindness is never weak but instead shows its strength by refusing to take revenge.

Kindness is its own reward. It brings us closer to God, who is the Supreme Good. It helps us to think like Him, to see our lives in the light of His loving plan for each one of us, and enables us to delight in life's daily joys. Kindness helps us through our difficulties and our struggles. Kindness is more rewarding than money, because money will always disappoint us. We were created to receive God's love and give it in our turn, not to measure everything in terms of money or power, which is a danger that threatens us all.

Address, April 21, 2014

FORGIVENESS IS NOT ALMSGIVING

—

You can forgive. A wound can be healed, a wound can close. But often it leaves a scar. And a scar means "I have forgiven but not forgotten." Always forgive, yes, but when you forgive someone, don't act as if you're giving them alms. No! Forgiveness comes from the heart. I have to simply begin to treat that person as if nothing happened . . . with a smile, and slowly forgiveness will come. True forgiveness doesn't happen on command: It takes an inner journey to forgive. It's not easy . . .

Meeting with Children and Young People, January 15, 2017

YOUR HOPE NEEDS
A BODY TO SUSTAIN IT

—

To be nourished, hope **needs a "body"** where all the different limbs support and revive one another. If we hope, it is because our brothers and sisters have taught us to hope and have kept our hope alive. I speak particularly of **the small ones, the poor, the simple,** and **the marginalized** here. Yes, because people who focus only on their own well-being do not truly know hope. They hope for themselves, and that is not hope: That is relative safety. He who thinks only of his own happiness, who always feels content, does not know hope. Instead, those who hope are those who are put to the test each day, who constantly face uncertainty and their own limitations. These brothers and sisters bear the strongest, most beautiful witness because they trust in the affection of Our Lord, and they know that beyond the sadness of oppression and the inevitability of death, the last word will be His, and it will be a word of mercy, of life, and of peace. Whoever hopes, hopes to one day hear this word: "Come, come to Me, brother; come, come to Me, sister, for all eternity."

General Audience, February 8, 2017

TO OBTAIN A FULL LIFE, INSPIRE, DO NOT JUST PUNISH

—

I remember once in a school there was a student who was an excellent soccer player but a terrible nuisance in the classroom. They gave him a rule that if he didn't behave well, he would have to stop playing soccer, which he enjoyed very much! He continued to behave badly, and so he had to stop playing soccer for two months. But this only made things worse. Be careful when you punish: Punishment made this boy worse. It's true. I met him, this boy. One day the coach spoke to the principal and told her, "This isn't working out. Let me try." He asked that the boy be allowed to play again. "Okay, we'll try that," the principal said. So the coach made him team captain. Then this child started to feel worthy, and he started to change for the better. He not only started to behave well, he improved across the board. This seems very important to me when it comes to education, very important. Some of our students are better at sports than they are at science, and others are better at art than at mathematics, and others are better at philosophy than sports. A good teacher, educator, or coach knows how to bring out the best qualities in the students without overlooking the other qualities.

Address, March 25, 2017

MAY YOUR COMMUNITY
BE BLESSED
—

Blessed are those Christian communities that live in authentic Gospel simplicity! Poor in means, they are rich in God. Blessed are the shepherds who pay no mind to worldly success, but follow the law of love: welcoming, listening, serving. Blessed is the Church that goes beyond functionality and organizational efficiency, beyond worries about her image.

Homily, October 1, 2016

LIVE A LIFE OF RECONCILIATION
—

A reconciled person sees in God the father of all, and as a consequence is spurred to feel brotherly love for all mankind. In Christ, the other is welcomed and loved as a son or daughter of God, as a brother or sister, not as a stranger, much less as a rival or even an enemy. In God's family, where all are sons and daughters of the same Father, and because they are grafted in Christ, **sons and daughters in the Son,** there are no "wasted lives." All men and women enjoy an equal and inviolable dignity.

Message for World Day of Peace, 2014

The Family, Life's Bounty

I take rest in the Lord with the
families, and remember my
own family: my father, my
mother, my grandfather, my
grandmother ...
ADDRESS, JANUARY 16, 2015

THE ANXIETY
OF THE SINGLE MAN

—

Jesus, in His reflection on marriage, refers us to a passage in Genesis, chapter 2, which paints a wonderful portrait of a couple, with the most splendid details. We will focus on just two of these. First, we see the man, who anxiously seeks "a helper suited to him" (verses 18

and 20), capable of alleviating the loneliness he feels despite being surrounded
by all of the animals, all of creation.
The original Hebrew suggests a direct
encounter, face to face, eye to eye, in a
kind of silent dialogue, for where love
is concerned, silence is always more
eloquent than words. It is an encounter with a face, a "thou" who reflects
God's love and is man's "richest treasure, a help like himself and a staunch
support," in the words of the biblical
sage (Sirach 36:29). Or as the bride
in the Song of Songs sings, in a beautiful avowal of love and mutual self-
bestowal: "My lover belongs to me and
I to him . . . I belong to my lover, and
my lover belongs to me" (2:16, 6:3).

From this encounter that heals loneliness arises the generations and the
family.

Amoris Laetitia 12

DOES YOUR FAMILY
STILL DREAM?

—

I am very fond of dreams in families. For nine months, every mother and father dreams about their baby. Am I right? They dream about what kind of child he or she will be . . . You can't have a family without a dream. When a family loses the ability to dream, children do not grow, love does not grow, life is stifled and shriveled. So I recommend that each evening, when you examine your conscience, you ask yourselves this question: Did I dream about my children's future today? Did I dream about the love of my husband, my wife, today? Today I dreamed about my parents, and my grandparents who came before me. Dreaming is very important. Especially dreaming in families. Don't lose your ability to dream!

Address, January 16, 2015

A FULL HUMAN BEING COMES FROM "ONE FLESH"

—

Adam, the original Everyman, with his wife creates a new family. Jesus speaks of this by quoting the passage from Genesis: "A man shall . . . be joined to his wife, and the two shall become one flesh" (Matthew 19:5; Genesis 2:24). The very phrase "to be joined," in the original Hebrew, suggests a profound harmony, a physical and spiritual bond of such depth that the same word is used to describe our union with God: "My soul clings fast to you" (Psalms 63:9). Marriage thus evokes not only a sexual and bodily union, but also a total gift of oneself, made in a spirit of love. The result of this union is that the two "become one flesh," both through their physical embrace and through the joining of their hearts and lives, and perhaps through a child, who will share not only genetically but also spiritually in the "flesh" of both parents.

Amoris Laetitia 13

LET LOVE BECOME THE NORM

Every Christian family can welcome Jesus—as Mary and Joseph did—by listening to Him, speaking with Him, guarding Him, protecting Him, and growing with Him; and thus every family can improve the world. Let us make room in our hearts and in our days for the Lord. Mary and Joseph did this, though it was not easy for them: Think of how many difficulties they had to overcome! They were a real family, not a fictional family. The family of Nazareth urges us to rediscover the purpose and the mission of the family, of every family. And what happened in those thirty years in Nazareth can happen to us, too. We, too, can make love—not hate—the norm. We, too, can make a helping hand—not indifference or enmity—commonplace.

General Audience, December 17, 2014

DON'T REDUCE COMMITMENT TO A SYSTEM OF BARTER

—

Freedom of choice makes it possible to shape our own lives and become our best selves. But if this freedom lacks noble goals or personal discipline, it degenerates into an inability to truly and generously give ourselves to another. Indeed, in many countries where the number of marriages is decreasing, more and more people are choosing to live alone—or simply spend time together without cohabiting. Freedom of choice has fostered a praiseworthy concern for justice, yes; but if misdirected, it can turn compatriots into clients out to claim the benefit of services rendered.

Amoris Laetitia 33

COME TO ME, FAMILIES, AND I WILL RESTORE YOU!

—

Dear families, the Lord knows our struggles. He knows them! He knows what weighs us down. But the Lord also knows our great desire to find joy and rest! Remember? Jesus said, "that your joy may be complete" (John 15:11). Jesus wants our joy to be complete! He said this to the Apostles and He says this to us today. So this is the first thing I want to share with you tonight, and it is a saying of Jesus: Come to me, families from around the world—so says Jesus—and I will give you rest, so that your joy may be complete. Take this Word of Jesus home with you, carry it in your hearts, share it with your families. Jesus invites us to come to Him so that He may give us joy, so that He may give everyone joy.

Address, October 26, 2013

REDISCOVER THE JOY
OF HUGGING

—

The family—with its capacity for hugging and supporting one another; for mimicking and deciphering one another's glances and silences; for laughing and crying with people whom we did not choose but who are so important to us—is what helps us understand that communication is about **discovering and creating closeness**. When we lessen distances by growing closer and accepting one another, we experience gratitude and joy. Elizabeth's blessing comes from Mary's greeting and from the stirring of her child; this is followed by the beautiful Canticle of the **Magnificat,** in which Mary praises God's loving plan for Her and for Her people. A "yes" spoken with faith can have effects that go far beyond ourselves: It ripples out into the world.

Message, January 23, 2015

The family that prays together, stays together

—

Resting in prayer is especially important for families. It is in the family that we first learn how to pray. Don't forget: The family that prays together, stays together! This is important. There we come to know God, to grow as men and women of faith, to see ourselves as members of God's greater family, the Church. In the family we learn how to love, to forgive, to be generous and open, not closed and selfish. We learn to move beyond our own needs, to encounter others and share our lives with them. That is why it is so important to pray as a family! So important! This is also why families are so crucial to God's plan for the Church! To pray is to rest in the Lord. So you must pray together, as a family.

Address, January 16, 2015

THERE IS NO SUCH THING AS A PERFECT FAMILY; MAKE IT A SCHOOL FOR FORGIVENESS

—

The family is where—more than anywhere else—we experience our own **limits** and the limits of others. Living together day in and day out, we confront the problem of getting along, the big and small problems of coexistence. The perfect family doesn't exist, but we don't have to be afraid of imperfections, weakness, or even conflict—we just have to learn how to deal with these things constructively. In this way the family, where we keep loving one another despite our limits and sins, becomes a **school of forgiveness**.

Message, January 23, 2015

TELL YOUNG NEWLYWED COUPLES THAT THEIR LOVE IS BEAUTIFUL!

—

Spousal and familial love clearly reveal each person's yearning for a unique and long-lasting love. They reveal the ways in which trials, sacrifices, and crises that couples face together represent opportunities for growth in kindness, truth, and inner beauty. In marriage we give ourselves completely, without calculation or reserve, sharing everything through good times and bad times, trusting in God's Providence. This is something that the young can learn from their parents and grandparents. Marriage is a way to experience faith in God, mutual trust, profound freedom, and even holiness—because like marriage, holiness requires daily devotion and daily sacrifice! But there are problems in marriage: There are always different points of view, jealousy, quarrels. But we must tell newlyweds that they should always make up before the day ends. The Sacrament of Marriage is renewed in this act of peace after an argument, a misunderstanding, a hidden jealousy, even a sin. Making peace brings unity to the family. This is what we must tell young people, young couples: Though marriage is not an easy road, it is a very beautiful one, very beautiful. We have to say this!

Address, October 25, 2013

DON'T TRANSFORM THE GOSPEL INTO A HEAVY STONE TO BE CAST AT THE POOR

I would like to call attention to the plight of families crushed by dire poverty. Their destitution limits their lives in the most heartbreaking ways. Everyone has problems, but in a very poor home, these problems become even harder.

For example: If a mother has to raise her son on her own, whether because she has separated from his father or for some other reason, and needs to leave the child alone at home while she goes to work, the child can grow up exposed to every type of risk and obstacle to his personal growth. In these difficult situations, the Church should take special care and be prepared to offer understanding, comfort, and acceptance rather than immediately imposing a set of rules as if they were casting stones. This will only lead to people feeling judged and abandoned by the very Mother called to show them God's mercy. Rather than offering the healing power of grace and the light of the Gospel message, some want to "indoctrinate" the Gospel, transforming a light into "heavy stones to be cast at others."

Amoris Laetitia 49

A FAMILY WHO TEACHES ITS CHILDREN WELL IS A BLESSING TO THE WORLD

—

When families bring children into the world and teach them about faith, give them sound values, and teach them to contribute to society, these children are a blessing to the world. Families can become a blessing to the world! God's love is manifested in the way we love and is felt through the good works that we do. This is how we spread the Kingdom of Christ in this world. By doing this, we are faithful to the prophetic mission entrusted to us when we are baptized.

Address, January 16, 2015

THE IMPORTANCE OF WALKING HAND IN HAND

—

Sometimes I think about marriages that end after many years. "We didn't understand each other anymore . . . we drifted apart." Maybe they couldn't apologize to each other. Maybe they didn't know how to forgive. I always give this advice to newlyweds: "Argue as much as you like. Let the plates fly. But never end the day without making up! Never!" If married couples can learn to say: "I'm sorry, I was tired," or make a little gesture, that counts as peace. Then you carry on with life in the morning. This is a beautiful secret, and it prevents these painful separations. It is so important to walk together, hand in hand, without running ahead, without looking back at the past. And while you walk you chat, you get to know each other, you reveal yourselves to each other, you grow as a family. So ask yourselves: How are we walking?

Address, October 4, 2013

How beautiful is the relationship between man and woman!

—

The most beautiful, admirable, and problem-free families actively **communicate** the beauty and richness of the relationship between man and woman, between parents and children. It all begins with **bearing witness**. We do not fight to defend the past. Rather, we work patiently to build a better future and we have faith in the people around us.

Message, January 23, 2015

The mission of your family is to "make room for Jesus in the world"

—

"Nazareth," which means "she who keeps," is like Mary, who "kept all these things in Her heart" as the Gospel states (Luke 2:19, 51). Since that time, whenever a family keeps this same mystery, even if they are at the very edge of the world, the mystery of the Son of God and the mystery of Jesus who comes to save us are at work. He comes to save the world. And this is the great mission of the family: to make room for the coming of Jesus, to welcome Jesus within our families, within each relative: children, husband, wife, grandparents . . . Jesus is there. Welcome Him, so that your family can grow spiritually.

General Audience, December 17, 2014

THE WOMB, FAMILY TIES, AND YOUR MOTHER TONGUE

—

Even after we have come into the world, in some sense we are still in a "womb," that is to say, in a family. **A womb made up of different persons:** The family is "where we learn to live with others despite our differences" (**Evangelii Gaudium** 66). Notwithstanding differences of gender and age, family members accept one another because there is a bond between them. And the greater the breadth of these relationships, the greater the differences of age, the richer the world becomes. It is this **bond** that is at the root of **language,** which in turn strengthens the bond. We do not create our language; we can use it because we have received it. It is in the family that we learn to speak our **mother tongue,** that is, the language of our ancestors (2 Maccabees 7:25, 27). In the family we realize that others have come before us, they gave us life and in turn made it possible for us to give life: to do something good and beautiful. We can give because we have received. This virtuous circle is at the heart of the family's ability to grow, to communicate within itself and with others. More generally, it is the model for all communication.

Message, January 23, 2015

WHEN THE JOY OF YOUTH
COMFORTS AND CONSOLES
THE ELDERLY

—

Jesus says four times that Our Lady and Saint Joseph **wanted to do what was required by the Law of the Lord** (Luke 2:22, 23, 24, 27). Jesus's parents evidently find joy in keeping God's commandments. Yes, they feel the joy of following the Laws of the Lord! They are two newlyweds, they have just had their baby, yet the desire to follow God's Law still animates them. This is not for appearance's sake; it is not about feeling good, no! It's a strong desire, a deep desire, a joyous desire. That's what the Psalm says: "I find joy in the way of Your testimonies . . . For your Law is my delight" (Psalms 119:14, 77).

And what does Saint Luke say of the elderly? He points out, more than once, that **they were guided by the Holy Spirit**. He says Simeon was a righteous and devout man, awaiting the consolation of Israel, and that "the Holy Spirit was upon him" (2:25). He says that "it had been revealed to him by the Holy Spirit" that he should not see death before he had seen the Lord's Christ (verse 26), and finally that he went to the Temple "in the Spirit" (verse 27). He says Anna was a "prophetess" (verse 36), and that she was inspired by God and always "worshiped night and day with fasting and prayer" in the Temple (verse 37). In short, these two elders are full of life! They are full of life because they are animated by the Holy Spirit, they obey Him, they respond to His call . . .

And now comes the encounter between the Holy Family and the two representatives of the holy people of God. Jesus is at the center. It is He who orchestrates everything, who brings all of them to the Temple, the house of His Father.

This is a meeting between the young, who are full of the joy that comes from observing the Law of the Lord, and the elderly, who are full of the joy of the Holy Spirit. It is **a unique encounter between observance and prophecy,** where the young people are the observers and the elderly are the prophets! In fact, if we think carefully, observance of the Law is animated by the Spirit, and prophecy moves forward according to the path laid down by the Law. Is there anyone more suffused with the Holy Spirit than Mary? Is there anyone more obedient to Its command?

Homily, February 2, 2014

VISIT OTHERS, OPEN DOORS, DON'T CLOSE YOURSELF IN, COMFORT OTHERS . . .

—

"Visiting" means opening your doors, not locking yourself away in your apartment. It is important to go out into the world, to go to the other. So, too, do the most dynamic families reach beyond themselves, breathing the world in. These families communicate a message of life and communion, and they give comfort and hope to families in distress, thus building up the Church herself, which is the family of families.

Message, January 23, 2015

TRANSFORM YOUR FAMILY INTO A STORY OF COMMUNION

The family is not an issue to debate or a battleground for ideological skirmishes. Rather, it is **an environment in which we learn to communicate,** a setting of kinship and closeness, a **"communicating community."** The family is a community that provides guidance, which flourishes and celebrates life together. Seen this way, it's clear that the family continues to be a rich human resource, as opposed to a problem or an institution in crisis. At times the **media** may present the family as a kind of abstract model that has to be accepted or rejected, defended or attacked, rather than a living, breathing reality. Or else it presents the family as grounds for ideological clashes rather than where we learn what it means to communicate, to receive love and to give love in return. We need to tell everyone that our lives intertwine to make one big story; that our voices are many, but that each one of us is unique.

Message, January 23, 2015

Successful Lives: When the Lord's Call Is Answered with Joy

***

Do not be afraid to show your
joy in having answered the
Lord's call, of having responded
to His choice of love and of
bearing witness to His Gospel.
MEETING WITH SEMINARIANS AND NOVICES,
JULY 6, 2013

A GLOOMY DISCIPLE IS A DISCIPLE OF GLOOM

***

Let's not be gloomy, disgruntled, or dissatisfied, for "a gloomy disciple is a disciple of gloom." Like all men and women, we have our troubles, our dark nights of the soul, our disappointments and illnesses; we, too, decline with old age. But in all these things we should be able to discover "perfect joy." We should be able to recognize the face of Christ, who was made in every respect like us, and rejoice in the knowledge that we are similar to Him who suffered on the Cross out of love for us.

In a society that worships efficiency, fitness, and success, that ignores the poor and dismisses "losers," we can bear witness to the truth of the words of Scripture: "When I am weak, then I am strong" (2 Corinthians 12:10).

Letter to All Consecrated People,
November 21, 2014

THE PLACE WHERE JOY IS BORN
—

I want to say one word to you, and that word is "joy." Wherever there are consecrated people, seminarians, religious men and women, and young people, there is joy! There is always joy! It is the joy of freshness, the joy of following

Jesus, the joy that the Holy Spirit gives us. There is joy! But—where is this joy born? For it is born ... On Saturday evening should I go home, or should I go out dancing with my old friends? Will joy be born from this? For a seminarian, for example? No? Or yes?

Meeting with Seminarians and Novices,
July 6, 2013

INFECTIOUS JOY AND ATTRACTION

The Church does not grow from proselytizing, but from attraction: the attraction of the joy of Jesus Christ, the testimony born from joy accepted and then transformed into proclamation. This is the foundational joy. Without this joy, without this happiness, we could not establish a Church! We could not establish a Christian community! This apostolic joy radiates and expands. Like Peter, I wonder: "Am I able to sit

next to my brother and slowly explain
the gift of the Word that I have received,
and infect him with my joy? Am I capable of conveying the enthusiasm of
those who discover the miracle of a new
life, which cannot be contained, which
demands docility because it draws us,
it entices us; and [of conveying] that
this new life is born from the encounter
with Christ?"

Homily, April 24, 2014

THE "NOSE" OF THE PEOPLE AND
THE NAME OF THE DOG

—

What could be more beautiful for us than
walking with our people? It is beautiful!
I think of the parish priests who know all
the names of their parishioners, who go
and visit them. One of them even told
me: "I know the name of each family's
dog." He even knew the dogs' names!
How wonderful is that! What could

be more beautiful? I say this often: We have to walk with our people, sometimes in front, sometimes beside them, sometimes behind: in front, to guide the community; beside them, for encouragement and support; and behind them, to keep everyone together and to make sure that no one lags too much. There is another reason, too: because the people have a "nose"! The people sniff out, discover, new paths, they have a **sensus fidei** [Latin: an intuition of the true faith], as the theologians call it. What could be more beautiful than this?

Address, October 4, 2013

OPEN YOUR HEART
TO NOBLE IDEALS

—

No calling creates itself or lives for itself. No, a calling flows from the heart of God and blossoms in the rich soil of the faithful, in the experience of brotherly love. Didn't Jesus say: "This is how all men will know that you are My disciples, if you have love for one another" (John 13:35)? . . . The true joy of those who are called consists in believing and experiencing that He, the Lord, is faithful, and that we can walk with Him, be His disciples and witnesses of His love, and open our hearts to noble ideals, to great things.

Message, May 11, 2014

Goodness is contagious

Saint Thomas said **"bonum est diffusivum sui"**—the Latin is not too hard!—Goodness radiates goodness, it spreads itself. And joy also spreads . . . Joy, true joy, is contagious; it is infectious . . . it pushes you forward. So if you meet a seminarian or novice who is a little too serious, too sad, you think: Something is wrong here! The joy of the Lord is missing, the joy that prompts you to serve, the joy of the encounter with Jesus: a joy that brings you, in turn, to encounter others to proclaim Him. This is missing! There is no holiness in sadness: There just isn't! Saint Teresa said: "A saint who is sad is a sad excuse for a saint." It's a little thing . . . but when you see a seminarian, a priest, a nun, or a novice with a long, gloomy face, it's like they've thrown a soaking wet blanket over themselves—you know, the really heavy kind, the kind that weighs you down, too . . . Something is wrong! Please, sisters and priests: no faces like "pickled peppers"—never!

Meeting with Seminarians and Novices,
July 6, 2013

IT IS NOT ENOUGH TO READ THE GOSPEL; YOU HAVE TO LIVE IT

—

We must ask ourselves this year whether—and how—we let ourselves be challenged by the Gospel; whether the Gospel is truly the "manual" for our daily life and for the choices we are asked to make. The Gospel is demanding: It demands to be lived radically and sincerely. It is not enough to read it (though the reading and study of Scripture are extremely important), it is not enough to meditate on it (which we do with joy every day). Jesus asks us to practice the Gospel, to live out His words.

Letter to All Consecrated People,
November 21, 2014

THE REAL PROBLEM OF CELIBACY IS BARRENNESS

—

Joy comes from Jesus. So when a priest—I say a priest, but it could be a seminarian, too—when a priest or a nun lacks joy, and he or she is sad, you might think: "Maybe it's a question of depression." It's true, this might be the case; mental illness can definitely happen, and some poor souls do have mental problems ... Certainly. But usually a lack of joy is not a psychological problem, it's a problem of dissatisfaction! And at the heart of this lack of joy? The issue of celibacy. Let me explain. You, seminarians, nuns, you consecrate your love to Jesus, a great love. Your heart is for Jesus, and this leads us to make the vow of chastity, the vow of celibacy. Once made, these vows of chastity and celibacy never end; rather, they endure ...

A consecrated life is a path that

grows, and grows, and grows into pastoral fatherhood, into pastoral motherhood. Thus when a priest is not a father to his community, when a nun is not a mother to all those with whom she works, he or she becomes sad. That is the real problem. This is why I say to you: The root of sadness comes from an absence of fatherhood or motherhood. This sadness comes from failing to live a truly consecrated life, which, on the contrary, always makes us fruitful, fertile. There is no such thing as a barren priest or nun: for this would not be Catholic! The beauty of consecration is joy, always joy . . .

Meeting with Seminarians and Novices,
July 6, 2013

THE GIFT OF A TRUE PRIEST

Priestly joy is a priceless treasure, not just for the priest but for all the faithful people of God: the faithful people for whom he is anointed and whom he, in turn, is sent to anoint.

A priest is anointed with the oil of joy so that he himself may anoint with the oil of joy. Priestly joy has its source in our Father's love, the Lord who wishes the joy of His love to be "ours" and to be "complete" (John 15:11). The priest is the poorest of men unless Jesus enriches him with His poverty; the most useless of servants unless Jesus calls him friend; the most ignorant of men unless Jesus patiently teaches him as He taught Peter; the frailest of Christians unless the Good Shepherd strengthens him through his own flock. No one is "smaller" than a priest left to his own devices; and therefore our prayer for protection against the insidiousness of the Evil One is the prayer of our Mother: I am a priest because He has looked with kindness upon my smallness (Luke

1:48). In that smallness we find our joy: our delight in our littleness!

Homily, April 17, 2014

THE ESSENCE OF A PRIEST LIES BEYOND HIMSELF

—

Many people, when they speak of the crisis of priestly identity, do not take into account that identity presupposes belonging. The priest who tries to find his priestly identity through introspection and soul-searching may well find signs telling him to "go forth," signs that say: Go outside yourself, go out in search of God. Go out and give your people what you yourself were given, for your people will make you feel and relish who you are, your name, your identity; they will make you rejoice in that hundredfold which the Lord has promised to those who serve Him. Unless you go beyond yourself, the oil will grow rancid and the anointing cannot be fruitful. Going outside of oneself requires self-effacement, requires shedding your ego, requires poverty.

Homily, April 17, 2014

LIVE WITH PASSION
IN THE PRESENT

—

Living with passion in the present means becoming "experts in communion," witnesses and architects of God's "plan for communion" that is, according to Him, the culmination of all human history. In a polarized society, where different cultures struggle to live alongside one another, where the weakest are oppressed, and where inequality abounds, we are called to offer a concrete model of community: a model that, by recognizing the dignity of each person and pooling our individual gifts, makes it possible to live as brothers and sisters.

Therefore, be men and women of communion! Have the courage to be present in the midst of conflict and tension, to be a credible sign of the presence of the Spirit that inspires in human hearts a passion for all to join as one (John 17:21).

Letter to All Consecrated People,
November 21, 2014

Marked by a passion for the Kingdom

—

Humanity urgently needs Christ's salvation. His disciples are those who allow the love of Jesus to seize them. They are marked by their fervent passion for the Kingdom of God. They are the bearers and the proclaimers of the joy of the Gospel. All the Lord's disciples are called to nurture this joy of evangelization.

The bishops are primarily responsible for this proclamation, and they have the task of supporting local churches in their missionary efforts. Bishops must always bear in mind that the joy of Jesus Christ is evinced by a determination to proclaim Him in the most distant places, as well as by a constant outreach to the very edges of their own territory, where there are many poor people waiting for His message.

Message, June 8, 2014

SING A SONG OF HOPE

Let us accompany Jesus as He goes forth to meet His people, to be in the midst of His people. Let us go forth without the complaints of those who have forgotten how to prophesy, without the anxieties of those who have failed to follow the dreams of their elders, but with serenity and songs of praise. Not with apprehension but with patience, the patience of those who trust in the Holy Spirit, the Lord of dreams and prophecy. In this way, we share our belonging: the hymn that is born of hope.

Homily, February 2, 2017

WHERE THE PIOUS ARE, THERE IS JOY

—

Let us hope that what I said once will always be true: "Where the pious are, there is joy." We are called to feel and show that God can fill our hearts to the brim with happiness. We are called to show that we need not seek our happiness elsewhere. We are called to show that the authentic fraternity found in our communities nourishes our joy. We are called to show that our total devotion to the Church, to families, young people, the elderly, and the poor, brings us lifelong personal fulfillment.

Letter to All Consecrated People,
November 21, 2014

Jesus's Joy Is in Seeing Our Names Written in Heaven

—

Luke the Evangelist tells us that the Lord sent the seventy-two disciples two by two into cities and villages to proclaim that the Kingdom of God was near, and to prepare people to meet Jesus. After completing this mission of preaching, the disciples returned full of joy: Joy is a dominant theme of this first and unforgettable missionary experience. Yet the Divine Master told them: " 'Do not rejoice because the spirits are subject to you, but rejoice because your names are written in Heaven.' At that very moment, He rejoiced in the Holy Spirit, and said: 'I give you praise, Father . . . ' And, turning to the disciples in private, He said, 'Blessed are the eyes that see what you see' " (Luke 10:20–21, 23).

Here, Luke presents us with three scenes. First, Jesus speaks to His disciples, then He addresses the Father, and then once again He speaks to the disciples. Jesus wants to share His joy with the disciples, which was different from and greater than any joy they had previously experienced.

The disciples are **filled with joy,** they are excited about their power to free people from demons. Yet Jesus reminds them to celebrate the love they have received, not the power, "because your names are written in Heaven" (Luke 10:20). The disciples have experienced God's love, and they have been given the opportunity to share that love with others. It is this experience of the disciples—the experience of God's love—that is a cause for joyous gratitude in Jesus's heart. Luke saw this jubilation as a display of the Trinitarian communion: "Jesus rejoiced in the Holy Spirit" when He addressed the Father and praised Him. This moment of deep joy springs from Jesus's immense love for His Father, Lord of Heaven and Earth, who hid these things from the wise and learned and revealed them to the little children (Luke 10:21). God has both hidden and revealed, and in this prayer of praise it is what He reveals that stands out. What has God revealed and hidden? The mysteries of His Kingdom, the manifestation of Jesus's divine lordship, and the victory over Satan.

Message for World Mission Day,
June 8, 2014

THE CITIES ON THE HILL
—

Monasteries, communities, centers of spirituality, citadels, schools, hospitals, family shelters: These are all places that your creative charisma and charity have conceived and brought into being. Yet we require constant and continued creativity to continue to bring these places into being. These places should be the leaven, the yeast for a society inspired by the Gospel: They must become the "city on a hill," which testifies to the truth and the power of Jesus's words.

Letter to All Consecrated People,
November 21, 2014

GOD CALLS US TO LIBERATE OURSELVES AND OUR BROTHERS

—

Hearing and answering the Lord's call is not a private and intimate matter, fraught with momentary emotion. Rather, it is a specific, concrete, and total commitment that embraces the whole of our existence and compels us to serve and to help build God's Kingdom on earth. The Christian vocation, rooted in the contemplation of our Father's heart, thus drives us to liberate our brothers and sisters, especially the poorest among us. A disciple of Jesus has an infinite and endlessly open heart. Being close to the Lord never means fleeing this life or the real world. On the contrary, intimacy with the Lord requires constant interaction between communion and mission.

Message for World Day of Prayer for Vocations, March 29, 2015

THERE IS A LACK OF VOCATION WHERE THERE IS A LACK OF ENTHUSIASM

—

Many parts of the world are experiencing a dearth of vocations to the priesthood and the consecrated life. Often this is due to the absence of contagious, evangelizing fervor, with the result that these communities lack enthusiasm and thus fail to attract new priests. The joy of the Gospel is born of the encounter with Christ and from sharing with the poor. For this reason I encourage parish communities, associations, and groups to live an intensely fraternal life, grounded in love for Jesus and concern for the needs of the most disadvantaged. Wherever there is joy, enthusiasm, and a desire to bring Christ to others, genuine vocations arise. Among these vocations, we should not overlook those lay people called to serve as missionaries. There has been a growing awareness of the identity and the mission of the laity in the Church, as well as the recognition that they may have an increasingly important role in the spread of the Gospel. That is why it is important for them to receive the training necessary for an effective apostolic mission.

Message, June 8, 2014

WHERE THERE IS FRATERNAL LOVE, THERE IS GOD
—

Jesus lives and walks the paths of ordinary life in order to be close to everyone, beginning with those who have least, and to heal our infirmities and illnesses. I turn now to those who are inclined to listen to the voice of Christ that rings out in the Church and to understand what their own vocation is. I invite you to listen to and follow Jesus, to allow His words to transform you, because they "are spirit and life" (John 6:63). Mary, the Mother of Jesus and our own, also says to us: "Do whatever He tells you" (John 2:5). His words will encourage you toward a communal journey that is able to release the best energies in you and around you. A vocation is a fruit that ripens in a well-cultivated field of mutual love, a fruit that becomes mutual service in the context of an authentic ecclesiastical life. Remember, no vocation is born of itself or lives for itself. A vocation originates in the heart of God and sprouts in the soil of the faithful, in the experience of fraternal love. Did not Jesus say: "This is how all will know that you are My disciples, if you have love for one another" (John 13:35)?

Message for World Day of Prayer for Vocations, 2014

CHRIST THE SHEPHERD WORKS THROUGH PRIESTS

—

All who are called know that genuine and complete joy exists in this world: It is the joy of being taken from the people we love and being sent back to them as dispensers of the gifts and counsels of Jesus, the one Good Shepherd. Jesus has a deep compassion for the little ones and the outcasts of this earth, for those who are as tired and oppressed as sheep without a shepherd. He wants to bring others to His ministry, so that He can stay among us and work for the good of His people, through His priests.

Homily, April 17, 2014

REMEMBER YOUR FIRST LOVE

—

I invite you to immerse yourself in the joy of the Gospel and nourish a love that can illuminate your vocation and your mission. I urge each of you to make an inner pilgrimage, and try to remember that "first love" you felt when Lord Jesus Christ warmed your heart. Don't do it for sentimental reasons: Do it to continue living in joy. The disciple of the Lord lives in joy when he stands next to Him, when he does His will, when he spreads the faith, hope, and evangelical mercy.

Message, June 8, 2014

The Blessings and Challenges of Womanhood

The Apostles and disciples
find it harder to believe.
The women, not so.
GENERAL AUDIENCE, APRIL 3, 2013

A CHURCH WITHOUT WOMEN?

A Church without women is like the
twelve Apostles without Mary. The role
of women in the Church is more than
maternal, more than being the mother
of a family. It is much greater: Mary is
the Virgin, She is Our Lady, She is the
one who helps the Church grow! Think
about it, Our Lady is more important
than the Apostles! She is much more

important! The Church itself is feminine. She is **la Chiesa,** the Church, she is a bride, she is a mother. But the role of women in the Church must not only ... I don't know how to say this in Italian ... the role of women in the Church must not be limited only to being mothers, workers ... No! They are something more, something else entirely!

Press Conference, July 28, 2013

SHARING PASTORAL RESPONSIBILITIES

—

The Church recognizes the indispensable contribution that women make to society, their sensitivity, their intuition, and other distinctive skills that women, more than men, tend to possess. For example, the special attention that women bestow on others, an attention often—but not exclusively—expressed in maternity. I happily acknowledge how many women share pastoral responsibilities with priests, how they guide people, families, and groups and thoughtfully contribute to theological studies.

But we need to create even more opportunities for women in the Church. We need feminine genius in every aspect of society. So women must be guaranteed roles in the workplace and wherever important decisions are made, both within the Church and in social structures.

Evangelii Gaudium 103

THE ROLE OF WOMEN IS NOT ONE OF SERVITUDE

—

I suffer—I really do—when I see a woman's role in the Church or in Church organizations reduced to a kind of **servidumbre** [servitude in the shadows]. I don't know if that is how you say it in Italian. Do you understand what I mean? Servitude. We all serve, but servitude is something else. When I see women reduced to acts of servitude, it is because others do not understand what women are capable of. How can we increase the role that women have within the Church?

Address, October 12, 2013

A POSSIBLE LIFE, AN INCOMPARABLE CONTRIBUTION

—

Many women feel that their rights, the value of their social and professional tasks, and their aspirations within the family and within society need better recognition. Some women are weary and nearly crushed by the volume of their many duties and tasks, by the lack of sufficient help and understanding. We must make sure that no woman is forced to take an exhausting job, to work too many hours. Such economic burdens only add to her responsibilities as homemaker and educator of her children. Above all, we must remember that a woman who cares for every aspect of her family life is making an incomparable contribution to the future of our society.

Address, December 2, 2014

BUILDING RECIPROCITY

Even though some countries have made significant strides when it comes to recognizing women's rights and their right to participate in public life, there is still room for improvement. Many unacceptable customs still exist. I think particularly of the shameful violence against women, both domestic violence and various forms of subjugation. These are not demonstrations of masculine power. They are cowardly acts of degradation. The verbal, physical, and sexual violence that women endure in some marriages contradicts the very nature of the conjugal union. I think of the reprehensible act of genital mutilation of women practiced in some cultures, as well as their lack of equal access to decent jobs and decision-making roles. History is rife with an excess of patriarchal cultures, cultures in which women are second-class citizens. Yet we must not overlook the use of surrogate mothers that exists today, and the exploitation and commercialization of the female body in the current media culture. There are those who believe that many of today's problems are a result of women's emancipation. This argument, however, is not valid, it is a falsehood, it is not true. It is a kind of male chauvinism. The equal dignity of men and women makes us happy to see old forms of discrimination disappear, to see the growth of equality within families. If certain forms of feminism are not in keeping with this growth of equality, we must nonetheless see the women's movement as the Holy Spirit working for a clearer recognition of the dignity and rights of women.

Amoris Laetitia 54

GOD ENTRUSTED HUMAN BEINGS TO WOMEN!

—

God entrusts humanity, all human beings, to the woman.

What is the meaning of this "entrustment"? It seems obvious to me that my predecessor refers to motherhood.*

Many things can change and have changed as our cultures and societies have evolved, but the fact remains that it is woman who conceives, who carries in her womb, and who gives birth to the children of men. This is not merely

---

*Pope Francis is referring to John Paul II, who wrote the first Papal Magisterium on the subject of women (**Mulieris Dignitate**) and who said that God "entrusts" man to woman.

a biological fact; it has many implications for a woman, for her way of being, for her relationships, for her relation to human life, and indeed for life in general. In calling woman to motherhood, God has entrusted the human being to her in an entirely special way.

Address, October 12, 2013

WOMEN AND MEN SHOULD COMPLEMENT EACH OTHER

—

Complementarity is the bedrock of marriage and family. The family is where we first learn to appreciate our talents and the talents of others, the school where we learn the art of living together. For most of us, the family is where we begin to absorb values and ideals, where we develop our capacity for virtue and charity. At the same time, we all know that our families can be a source of tension: between egoism and altruism, between reason and passion, between immediate desires and long-term goals, and so on. Crucially, families also provide an arena for resolving these tensions. But we must not confuse complementarity with the simplistic idea that the roles and relationships of men and women can be confined to a single, static model. Complementarity takes many forms, since every man and every woman makes his or her own contribution—whether it be wealth or richness of personality—to their marriage and to the upbringing of their children. Thus complementarity becomes a great treasure—it is not only an asset but also a thing of beauty.

Address, November 17, 2014

Two dangers that threaten the vocation of women

There are two ever-present dangers, two opposing extremes that threaten a woman and her vocation. The first is the reduction of motherhood to a social role, to a noble task that sets the woman and her potential aside and does not appreciate her ability to build a community. This happens both in civil and ecclesiastical circles. Then there is the second danger, which is a reaction to the first and lies at the opposite end of the spectrum. In this form of emancipation, the woman assumes roles that have been copied from the male domain and that ignore the precious feminine traits that characterize womanhood.

Address, October 12, 2013

WHAT FEMALE GENIUS CAN CONTRIBUTE TO FAMILIES, SOCIETY, AND THE CHURCH

Whether women's talents are more important to the business world or the public sphere, women are, without a doubt, essential to the family. For

Christians, the family is more than a private place; it is a domestic church, whose health and prosperity are necessary for the health and prosperity of the Church and of society itself. Let us think of Our Lady: The Madonna creates something that priests, bishops, and popes cannot create. She is the true feminine genius. Let us think about Our Lady in families—about what the Madonna does within a family. The presence of women in the domestic sphere is more necessary than ever, both for inculcating sound moral principles and for teaching the faith to future generations.

Address, January 25, 2014

LEARN FROM THE WOMEN OF THE RESURRECTION TO GO OUT AND SHARE THE FAITH!

—

The first witnesses of the Resurrection were the women. At dawn they went to the tomb to anoint Jesus's body and found the first sign: the empty tomb (Mark 16:1). Their meeting with a messenger of God followed. This messenger announced: "Jesus of Nazareth, the Crucified. He has been raised; He is not here" (Mark 16:5–6). The women were motivated by love and were able to accept this announcement with faith: They believed and passed it on straightaway; they did not keep it to themselves but passed it on.

They could not contain their joy, their knowledge that Jesus was alive, or the hope that filled their hearts. This should happen for us, too. Let us feel the joy of being Christian! We believe in the Risen One who conquered evil and death! Let us have the courage to "come out of ourselves" to bring this joy and this light to every aspect of our lives! The Resurrection of Christ is our greatest certainty; He is our most precious treasure! How can we not share this treasure, this certainty, with others? It is not only for us, it is to be passed on, to be shared.

General Audience, April 3, 2013

THEOLOGICAL WORK BY WOMEN SHEDS LIGHT ON THE UNKNOWABLE

—

I invite you to reflect on the role that women can and must have in theology . . . By virtue of their feminine genius, women theologians can detect, to the benefit of all, previously unexplored aspects of the unfathomable mystery of Christ "in whom are hidden all the treasures of wisdom and knowledge" (Colossians 2:3). I invite you to take advantage of the unique contribution women can make to our understanding of the faith.

Address, December 5, 2014

Always bear witness!

This is part of the mission of women—of mothers—of all women! To bear witness to your children and grandchildren that Jesus is alive, that He is living, that He has risen. Mothers and women: Keep bearing witness to this! For it is our hearts that matter to God, how open our hearts are to Him, whether we are as trusting as children.

This also reflects how women, in the Church and on the journey of faith, had and still have a special role in opening the doors to the Lord, in following Him and in communicating His Face to others. For the look of faith always needs the simple and profound look of love.

General Audience, April 3, 2013

RISKY CHOICES CAN BE MADE
BY WOMEN

—

In the Church, we should think of women as capable of making risky decisions. This needs to be better explained. I think that we still lack a profound theology of womanhood in the Church. All we say is: They can do this, they can do that, now they are altar servers, now they do the readings, they are in charge of Caritas [Catholic charities] . . . But there is more! We need to develop a profound theology of womanhood. That is what I think.

Press Conference, July 28, 2013

WOMEN, NOT MEN,
ARE THE TRUE CHAMPIONS

—

Women have an ability to give life and to bestow tenderness, peace, and joy that we men do not have. There is only one model for you: Mary, the woman of faith, who didn't understand what was happening but obeyed. The woman who ran to Her cousin when She found out what Her cousin needed from Her; She was the Virgin of Readiness. She was the one that escaped to a foreign country to save Her Son's life. She was the one who helped Her Son grow and who, when Her Son began to preach, followed Him. She was the one who endured, through everything that happened to Her Child, to the Young Man. She was beside Her Son and told Him what the problems were: "Look, there is no wine." The one who, at the moment on the Cross, was there next to Him . . .

May Mary, Our Lady of Consolation, Our Lady of Tenderness, Our Lady of Readiness, always ready to serve, guide you on your path. Women, try not to be angry, for it has been proven that you, not men, are the champions.

Videomessage, April 26, 2014

An unforgettable
female icon
—

When the sins of the world encountered God's divine mercy, when Christ suffered on the Cross, He could feel the consoling presence of His Mother and His friend at His feet. At that crucial moment, before finishing the mission His Father had entrusted to Him, Jesus said to Mary: "Woman, behold, your son." Then He said to His beloved friend: "Behold, your Mother" (John 19:26–27). These words of the dying Jesus are not chiefly the expression of His devotion and concern for His Mother; rather, they are a revelation that manifests the mystery of a special salvific mission. Jesus left us His Mother so that she would become our mother. Only after doing so did Jesus know that "everything was now finished" (John 19:28). At the foot of the Cross, at the supreme hour of the new creation, Christ led us to Mary. He led us to Her because He wanted us to have a mother, so that we could read in this maternal image all the mysteries of the Gospel. The Lord did not want to leave His Church without this icon of womanhood.

Evangelii Gaudium 285

NO MACHISMO IN A SKIRT

It is necessary to expand the role of women in the Church. But I am wary of a "machismo in a skirt" solution because women and men are made very differently. So often, the ideas that I hear for expanding the role of women in the church are inspired by a macho ideology. Women are asking deep questions that must be addressed. The Church cannot exist without women and the roles they play. Women are essential to the Church. Mary, a woman, is more important than the bishops. I say this because we must not confuse function with dignity. So we must raise the profile of women in the Church. We need to work harder to develop a profound theology of the woman. By doing this we will be able to better reflect on their true capabilities. The feminine genius is needed wherever we make important decisions. So our challenge is this: to reflect on the specific roles women can have within the Church, areas where authority is wielded.

Interview with Father Antonio Spadaro,
August 19, 2013

PART III

A HUNDREDFOLD REWARD—PLUS SUFFERING

Beyond Tears and Loneliness

He who scalds himself with
milk, sees a cow and cries.
FOLK PROVERB

GOD IS PART OF OUR DAILY STRUGGLES

God takes the initiative and chooses to join us in our homes and enter into our everyday struggles, our anxieties, and our desires—just as He did with Mary. It is here in our cities, our schools and universities, in our town squares and hospitals, that we can hear the most beautiful message of all: "Rejoice, the Lord is with you!" The joy of the Lord generates life and creates hope. This joy is made flesh, is manifested in our vision for the future, our attitude toward others. This joy becomes the solidarity, generosity, and mercy we show to all.

Homily, March 25, 2017

EVEN THE POPE HAS HIS FEARS

Q. I am afraid of some things. What are you afraid of?

A. (**Pope Francis**) Of myself! Fear . . . Look, in the Gospel, Jesus often says, "Don't be afraid! Don't be afraid!" He says it many times. Why? Because He knows that fear is—you could say—a normal thing. We are afraid of life, we are afraid of the challenges we face, we are afraid of God . . . Everyone is afraid. But you shouldn't worry about being afraid. You should ask, "Why am I afraid?" Before God and for yourself, you must try to understand the situation or ask someone for help.

Fear is not a good counselor; he gives you bad advice. He pushes you down the wrong path. This is why Jesus said, "Don't be afraid! Don't be afraid!" We have to know ourselves. Everyone has to know himself or herself, has to know the places where they might slip up; we need to be a little afraid of those places. Because there is good fear and bad fear. Good fear is like prudence. It's prudent to think: "Look, you are weak at this, this, and this; be careful and don't fall." Bad fear is the kind that undermines you, that crushes you, that holds you back. This is bad fear, and you must cast it out.

Meeting with Young People,
March 31, 2014

THE GOSPEL IS NOT SKIN-DEEP!

—

Jesus has risen! We have seen Him!
Let us allow this experience, one in-

scribed in the Gospel, to be inscribed in our hearts and to light up our lives . . . If only we could be truly illuminated by its light! But this light goes deeper than the skin—it comes from within, from a heart immersed in the source of this joy, like that of Mary Magdalene, who wept over the loss of her Lord and could hardly believe her eyes when she saw He had risen. Whoever experiences this light becomes a witness of the Resurrection, for in a way he himself or she herself has also risen. He or she then shares the ray of light of the Risen One with those who are happy, thereby making them more beautiful by preserving them from selfishness; and with those who are in pain, bringing them serenity and hope.

Regina Coeli, April 21, 2014

WHEN THE DEVIL
IS DISGUISED AS AN ANGEL
—

There is one word that I want to say to you: **joy**! Never be sad, men and women: A Christian should never be sad! Never let yourself be discouraged! Our joy does not come from owning many things, but from having met someone—Jesus, who is among us. Our joy is born from knowing that with Him we are never alone, even in the most difficult moments, even when our problems threaten to overwhelm our path through life. Even when we are facing a multitude of apparently insurmountable obstacles! It is at this moment that the enemy—the Devil—comes to us, often disguised as an angel, and slyly speaks to us. Don't listen to him! We follow Jesus! We walk with and follow Jesus—and above all, we know that He walks with us and carries us on His shoulders. This is our joy; this is the hope that we must bring to this world. Please do not let yourselves be robbed of this hope! Do not let what Jesus gave be taken from you!

Homily, March 24, 2013

WHEN WE LIVE AMONG THE THORNS AND IN THE DESERT

—

It often seems as if the seeds of goodness and hope that we sow are smothered by the weeds of selfishness, hostility, and injustice—not only around us, but in our own hearts, too. We are troubled by the growing gap between the rich and the poor in our societies. We see how the false idols of wealth, power, and pleasure are worshipped, and at what cost to humanity. We see many of our friends and contemporaries enjoying immense material prosperity, even as they suffer from spiritual poverty, loneliness, and quiet despair. It almost seems as if God is out of the picture. It is as if a spiritual desert is spreading throughout the world, a desert that also robs the young of hope and, too often, of life itself. Yet this is the world in which you are called to go to witness the Gospel of hope, the Gospel of Jesus Christ, and the promise of His Kingdom.

Address, August 15, 2014

WELCOME THE CHALLENGE OF TEARS

The world of today lacks tears! The marginalized weep, those who are neglected weep, the scorned weep, but those of us who have a relatively comfortable life, we don't know how to weep. But certain harsh realities can only be seen by eyes that have been cleansed by tears. Ask yourselves: Have I learned to weep? Do I weep when I see a hungry child, a child on drugs, a homeless child, an abandoned child, an abused child, or a child used as a slave by society? Or are my tears the selfish tears of someone who wants something for himself? This is the first thing I would like to say to you: We must learn to weep . . .

In the Gospel, Jesus wept. He wept for His dead friend. He wept in His heart for the family that lost its son. He wept in His heart when He saw the poor widowed mother burying her son. He was moved and He wept in His heart when He saw the crowds behave like sheep without a shepherd. If you do not learn to weep, you are not a good Christian. This is your challenge.

Address, January 18, 2015

THE PATH OF RUIN AND THE PATH OF FULFILLMENT

—

How much families suffer when one of their own—often a young person—is enslaved by alcohol, drugs, gambling, or pornography! How many people have lost their purpose in life or their prospects for the future! How many have lost hope! How many people are plunged into misery by social injustice, by unemployment—which robs people of their dignity, their pride in being breadwinners—and by lack of equal access to education and health care. This moral misery, this destitution, pushes people to the brink: They are imminent suicides. The destitution caused by financial ruin is akin to the spiritual destitution that strikes us when we turn away from God and reject His love. If we think we don't need God, who reaches out to us through Christ—if we believe we can make do on our own—we are on the path to ruin. God alone can truly save and free us.

Message for Lent, 2014

Beware a senseless solitude

The great danger in today's world, overwhelmed as it is by an all-pervading consumerism, is the desolation and anguish born of a complacent yet covetous heart; the feverish pursuit of frivolous pleasures; a blunted conscience. Whenever we are immersed in ourselves, there is no room for other people. We do not consider the poor. We no longer hear God's voice, no longer feel the quiet joy of His love, and our desire to do good fades. This is a very real danger for believers, too. Many people fall into this trap and become resentful, disgruntled, and listless. That is no way to live a dignified and fulfilled life; it is not what God wants for us, nor is it in keeping with the Spirit that flows from the heart of the Risen Christ.

Evangelii Gaudium 2

THE ULTIMATE MEANING
OF YOUR EXISTENCE
COMES FROM GOD

—

The first kind of indifference in human society is indifference to God, which then leads to indifference to one's neighbor and to all of creation. Combined with relativism and nihilism, this indifference is one of the gravest consequences of false humanism and materialism. Man thinks that he is the source and creator of himself, his life, and his society. We feel self-sufficient, prepared not only to replace God but to eliminate Him. As a result, we think only of ourselves, and we demand whatever we think we are entitled to.

Message for World Day of Peace, 2016

How is my mind changing?

—

Is your mindset—in Latin, your **forma mentis**—more self-absorbed, or more considerate of others? If it is more considerate, that is a good sign, because although you are going against the grain, you are going in the only direction that has a future and that offers a future. True solidarity with others, which is not declared but rather experienced concretely, creates peace and hope for all countries and for the whole world.

Address, February 17, 2017

May your Lent flow into Easter

—

There are Christians whose lives seem like Lent without Easter. I realize that we do not experience joy in the same way in every phase of life—particularly in moments of great difficulty. Joy adapts and changes, but it always endures, even as a tiny glimmer of light. It is a light born of our certainty that we are infinitely loved. I understand the grief of those who have endured great suffering, but we must let the joy of faith awaken within us as a quiet yet firm trust, even amid the greatest distress.

Evangelii Gaudium 6

GOD IS NOT INSENSITIVE, BUT CAIN IS. HOW ABOUT YOU?

—

Cain said that he didn't know what happened to his brother, he said he was not his brother's keeper. He did not feel responsible for his brother's life or for his fate. Cain was unperturbed. He was indifferent to his brother despite their shared origin. What a sad story—a family tragedy, a human tragedy! This was the first display of indifference between brothers. But God is not indifferent. Abel's blood is important to Him, and

He asked Cain to account for his actions. Since the earliest days of humanity, God has shown that He cares about the fate of mankind.

Message for World Day of Peace, 2016

ARE WE LIVING THROUGH THE GLOBALIZATION OF INDIFFERENCE?

—

God is not indifferent. Each one of us has a place in His heart. He knows us by name, He cares for us and seeks us out even if we turn away from Him. He is interested in all of us; His love does not allow Him to be indifferent to what happens to us. Usually, when we are healthy and feel comfortable, we forget about other people (which God the Father never does). We do not care about their problems, their pain, what injustices they endure ... Our hearts lapse into indifference: As long as **I** am relatively comfortable, I forget about those less well off. This selfish attitude has taken on global proportions, so much so that we can speak of a globalization of indifference. This is a problem that we, as Christians, must confront.

Message for Lent, 2015

AVOID ARTIFICIAL PARADISES

Our culture is dominated by technology, yet sadness and loneliness are on the rise, and not only among young people. The future seems riddled with uncertainty, which only adds to a general feeling of instability. This is how depression, sadness, and boredom are born; this is how despair begins. We need witnesses of hope and true joy if we are to dispel the chimeras, the illusions that promise easy happiness through artificial paradises. Profound emptiness can be dispelled by heartfelt hope, by the joy that we can bring to others, the joy that rises up in a heart touched by mercy. Let us keep in mind, then, the words of the Apostle: "Rejoice in the Lord always" (Philippians 4:4; see also 1 Thessalonians 5:16).

Misericordia et Misera 3

DON'T BE AFRAID OF LOVE

—

Youth is a time of life when your desire for love—one that is genuine, beautiful, and expansive—begins to blossom. How powerful this capacity for love is! But you must not let this precious treasure be distorted, destroyed, or spoiled. This can happen if we use our neighbors for our own selfish needs, as mere objects of pleasure. Hearts are broken and remain sad after these negative experiences. I urge you: Do not be afraid of true love, the love that Jesus teaches us and that Saint Paul describes as "patient and kind." Saint Paul says, "Love is patient, love is kind. It is not jealous, it is not pompous, it is not inflated, it is not rude, it does not seek its own interests, it is not quick-tempered, it does not brood over injury, it does not rejoice over wrongdoing but rejoices in the truth. It bears all things, believes all things, hopes all things, endures all things" (1 Corinthians 13:4-8).

Message for World Youth Day,
January 31, 2015

ACCEPT THE CHALLENGE TO RESTORE DIGNITY TO HUMANITY
—

Being unemployed or receiving an insufficient salary; lacking a home or a homeland; being discriminated against because of one's faith, race, or social status: These are just a few examples of attacks on human dignity. In the face of such attacks, Christian mercy responds with vigilance and solidarity. There are many ways to restore human dignity to individuals! Think of all the children subjected to violence, violence that robs them of the joy of life. Their sad and bewildered faces are imprinted in my mind; they are pleading for our help, they want to be set free from modern-day slavery. These children are the adults of tomorrow. Are we preparing them for lives of dignity and responsibility? What hope do they have for their present, for their future?

Misericordia et Misera 19

LIVE YOUR COMPASSION; DON'T LET YOURSELF BE DISCOURAGED

—

We always hear about people who succumb to despair and do bad things . . . Desperation drives them to brutality. This happens to people who are discouraged, who are weak, who feel weighed down by life, by the burden of their sins. They cannot pick themselves up. The Church must be closer, warmer, more intense in its love for these people. We must demonstrate the most exquisite form of compassion, which goes beyond sympathy: Compassion means suffering with those who are suffering, suffering alongside them, staying close to them and drawing them in. "Compassion" is a kind word, spoken from the heart; it is offering your hand to someone who needs comfort and consolation. Compassion is more important than ever: Christian hope cannot do without such genuine and tangible charity.

General Audience, February 8, 2017

BE THE EYES OF THE BLIND AND THE FEET OF THE LAME

—

How many Christians today show—not with words but with lives rooted in faith—that they are "eyes to the blind" and "feet to the lame"? How many Christians stay close to sick people who are in need of constant care, how many help them to wash, dress, and eat? This service, especially when it is long-term, can become tiring and burdensome. It is relatively easy to help someone for a few days, but it is difficult to look after a person for months or even years—especially if this person can no longer express their gratitude. Yet how blessed such service is!

Message for World Day of the Sick, 2015

PRAY FOR HEALTH, BUT ALSO FOR PEACE

The tenderness of God is reflected in Mary's concern for others. This same tenderness is present in the lives of those people who care for the sick and understand all of their needs, even the smallest and subtlest ones, because their eyes are full of love. How many times has a mother prayed to Our Lady at the bedside of her sick child, or a child prayed to Mary when caring for an elderly parent, or a grandchild prayed for a grandparent! We always ask for the health of our loved ones. Jesus Himself demonstrated the presence of the Kingdom of God through healing: "Go and tell John what you hear and see: The blind regain their sight, the lame walk, lepers are cleansed, the deaf hear, the dead are raised, and the poor have the Good News proclaimed to them" (Matthew 11:4–5). Love animated by faith makes us ask for something greater than physical health: We ask for peace, for the serenity that comes from the heart. This peace is a gift from God, it is the fruit of the Holy Spirit that the Father never denies to the faithful.

Message for World Day of the Sick, 2016

WE LIKE OUR IDOLS . . .

—

Faith means trusting in God. Those who have faith trust in God. But sometimes in life, in difficult times, man experiences the fragility of that trust and wants tangible, concrete assurances. I entrust myself to God, but this situation is pretty serious and I'd like a little more certainty. Therein lies the danger! That's when we are tempted to seek fleeting, short-lived comforts, when we search for something to fill the void inside us, assuage our loneliness, and alleviate the hard work of belief. We think we can find these comforts in money, in alliances with the powerful, in worldliness, in false ideologies. Sometimes we look for a god who will bow to our demands and magically intervene to change reality, to make it what we wish: a helpless and deceitful idol that has no power. But we like these idols; we like them very much!

General Audience, January 11, 2017

Don't chase trends, don't "test drive" love

—

Some people say "joy comes from possessions," so they go after the latest smartphone, the fastest motorcycle, the showiest car. But I tell you, it truly grieves me to see a priest or a nun driving the latest model of a car: No! It's wrong! It's really wrong! Perhaps you are thinking, "So now we have to get around by bicycle, Father?" . . . Bicycles are good! Monsignor Alfred rides a bicycle. He gets around by bike. I believe that cars are necessary, especially if you have a lot of work to do, if you have to get about . . . but choose a humble car! And if you like a beautiful one, just think of all the children who are dying of hunger. Just think! Joy does not come from things we possess! Others say that joy comes from the extreme, from the thrill of an adrenaline rush: Young people especially like to walk on the edge of a knife! Still others like trendy clothes or going to the most fashionable places—I'm not saying that nuns go to those places, I'm talking about young people in general. Others say that joy comes from success with the ladies or success with men, from constantly changing your boyfriend or girlfriend. This is insecurity in love, it's uncertainty. It's "test driving" love. We could go on . . . You see this reality; you, too, cannot ignore it.

Meeting with Seminarians and Novices,
July 6, 2013

MAY THE WATER OF YOUR LIFE BECOME PRECIOUS WINE

—

Whether we are healthy or sick, we can offer up our toil and suffering as if it were the water that filled the jars at the wedding feast of Cana, which was turned into the finest wine. By quietly helping those who suffer, those who are ill, we take our daily cross upon our shoulders and follow the Master (Luke 9:23). Even though the experience of suffering will always remain a mystery, Jesus helps us to reveal its meaning.

If we can learn to obey the words of Mary, who says, "Do whatever He tells you," Jesus will always transform the water of our lives into precious wine.

Message for World Day of the Sick, 2016

THE DOORS OF CONSOLATION

If we want to experience the comfort of the Lord, we must make room for the Lord in our lives. In order for the Lord to live within us, we must open the doors of our hearts. The **doors of consolation** must always be open; Jesus loves to enter through them. The Gospel we read every day and carry around with us, our silent prayers, Confession, the

Eucharist: These are the doors through which the Lord enters our hearts, infusing all things with light. But when the doors of our heart are closed, His light cannot enter and everything remains dark. That's when we resign ourselves to pessimism, to negativity, to situations that never change. We are locked inside ourselves, trapped in our sadness, entombed in our anguish. If, on the other hand, we throw open the doors of consolation, the Lord's light enters!

Homily, October 1, 2016

STRENGTHEN THE ROOTS
OF YOUR HOPE

—

Hope is a gift from God. We must ask for it. Hope is located deep within each human heart in order to illuminate life, because our lives are so often troubled and obscured by sadness and pain. We need to nourish the roots of our hope so that our hope can bear fruit: The first and most important fruit is the certainty of God's presence and His compassion, despite the evil we may do.

There is no corner of our heart that God's love cannot reach. When someone makes a mistake, the Father's mercy is all the more present, awakening repentance, forgiveness, reconciliation, and peace.

Homily, November 6, 2016

ARE YOU SUFFERING? KNOW JESUS, BUT NOT THROUGH SOMEONE ELSE!

—

Even when illness, loneliness, and disability make it hard for us to reach out to others, suffering can be a privilege, a way of discovering grace and the fountain of **sapientia cordis,** the wisdom of the heart. And so, we understand how Job, at the end of his ordeal, could turn to God and say, "By hearsay I had heard of You, but now my eye has seen You" (42:5). People immersed in the mystery of pain, when they accept their suffering with faith—even if they don't understand its full meaning—can become living witnesses of faith, and capable of embracing suffering.

Message for World Day of the Sick, 2015

LIGHTS THAT DAZZLE AND LIGHTS THAT ILLUMINATE

—

Life has many different kinds of lights, ones that sparkle and ones that guide. It is up to us to choose which ones to follow. For example, there are **flashing lights** that come and go, the small pleasures of life. Although they may be fun, they are not enough, because they do not last and they do not give us the peace we seek.

Then there is the **dazzling limelight**

of money, fame, and success; this light promises the world, and all at once. It is a seductive light, but its intensity blinds us. It is a light that begins in dreams of glory and fades into the darkest darkness. The Magi instead invite us to follow a **steady light,** a **gentle light** that never fades, because it is not of this world: It comes from Heaven and shines . . . where? In the heart.

This true light is the Lord's light, or rather, **it is the Lord Himself**. He is our light: He is a light that does not dazzle, He is a light that guides us and bestows a unique joy.

Angelus, January 6, 2017

If You Only Share Crumbs, You Won't Satisfy Hunger

—

It is easy to give up a part of your earnings without coming into contact with and embracing the people who receive those "crumbs." On the other hand, just five loaves of bread and two fish can feed a crowd—if you are sharing your whole life.

The logic of the Gospel is: He who does not give all of himself, never gives enough of himself.

Address, February 4, 2017

No wise man closes in on himself

Wisdom of the heart means going forth from ourselves toward our brothers and sisters. Occasionally we forget the special value associated with time spent at the bedside of the sick; we are always in a rush, so caught up in a frenzy of doing and of producing that we forget about giving ourselves freely, about taking care of others, and being responsible for others. Behind this attitude there is often only a lukewarm faith, one that has forgotten the Lord's words: "You did [it] for Me" (Matthew 25:40).

Message for World Day of the Sick, 2015

DO YOU WANT TO RESEMBLE GOD, OR THE IDOLS WHO "DO NOT SPEAK"?

—

Psalm 115 says:

Their idols are silver and gold,
The work of human hands.
They have mouths but do not
   speak;
Eyes but do not see.
They have ears but do not hear;
Noses but do not smell.
They have hands but do not feel;
Feet but do not walk;
They produce no sound from
   their throats.
Their makers will be like them;
And anyone who trusts in them!

verses 4–8

The psalmist presents to us, somewhat ironically, the ephemeral nature of these idols. We understand that idols are not merely physical figures constructed of metal or other materials, but things we build in our minds, either when we take limited realities and transform them into absolutes or when we reduce God to fit our own ideas about divinity. A god that looks like us is understandable and predictable, like the idols mentioned in the Psalm. When man, the image of God, manufactures a god in his own image, it is a poorly made image: It does not feel, it does not act, and above all, it cannot speak. But sometimes we are happier to turn to idols than to turn to the Lord . . .

The message of the Psalm is very clear: If you place your hope in idols, you become like them: empty images with hands that do not feel, feet that do not walk, a mouth that cannot speak. You no longer have anything to say; you become unable to help, to change things, unable to smile, to give of yourself, incapable of love. And we, men of the Church, run this risk when we become worldly. We need to live in the world but defend ourselves from the world's illusions, which are these idols that I mentioned . . .

This is the wonderful reality of hope: In trusting in the Lord, we become like Him.

General Audience, January 11, 2017

OUR OBSESSIONS

We distance ourselves from God's love when we incessantly search for earthly goods and riches, because in doing so we display a fondness for these objects, these things.

Jesus says that this frantic search is illusory and that it leads to unhappiness. He gives His disciples a fundamental precept: "Seek first and foremost the Kingdom of God." We must fulfill the plan that Jesus revealed in the Sermon on the Mount, entrusting ourselves to God, who never disappoints. Many friends, or many people who we believed were friends, have disappointed us, but God never disappoints! We must be dedicated and faithful stewards of the goods that He has given us, even the earthly goods, but without overdoing things. Nothing, not even our salvation, depends only on us. This evangelical attitude requires a clear choice, which today's reading indicates precisely: "You cannot serve God and mammon" (Matthew 6:24). It's either the Lord, or the fascinating but illusory idols. We are called on to make this choice, and it has an impact on our actions, our plans, and our commitments. We must choose clearly and continuously; the temptation to reduce everything to money, pleasure, and power is relentless. There are so many temptations of this kind.

Angelus, February 26, 2017

WHAT'S MORE IMPORTANT, YOU OR YOUR BEAUTY?

—

We either place our hope in the Lord who created the world and guides with His Word, or we turn to mute simulacra. Ideologies like wealth (this is a popular idol), power, success, vanity claim to understand the absolute and offer an illusion of eternity and omnipotence. They emphasize physical beauty and health. If they become idols, if we sacrifice everything for these things, our hearts and minds become confused and, instead of bringing us life, lead us to death. I heard something once, years ago, in the Diocese of Buenos Aires. It was terrible to hear, and brought pain to my soul. A good woman—who was very beautiful—was boasting about her beauty. She said, as if it were completely natural, "I had to have an abortion because my figure is very important to me." These are idols, and they lead you down the wrong path. They do not bring happiness.

General Audience, January 11, 2017

DON'T TRUST THE PEACE OF MIND THAT FORTUNE-TELLERS OFFER YOU

—

Once, in Buenos Aires, I had to go from one church to another. The distance was about a kilometer. I went on foot. I walked through a park, and in the park were many little tables, and at each one was a fortune-teller. The park was full of people, they were even waiting in line. You would give the fortune-tellers your hand and they'd begin, but they always said the same things: "There is a woman in your life, a darkness is coming but everything will be fine . . ." And then you paid. This gives you peace of mind? It is the security of—allow me to use the word—idiocy. Going to a fortune-teller or a tarot card reader: This is an idol! This is idolatry, and when we rely on these idols, we are buying false hope.

General Audience, January 11, 2017

HE WHO IS CORRUPT IS NOT HAPPY TODAY, NOR WILL HE BE IN THE FUTURE

—

Here I am thinking of people who are responsible for others and still let themselves be corrupted; do you think a corrupt person will be happy on the other side? No, all the fruit of his corruption has corrupted his heart, and it will be difficult for him to go to the

Lord. I am thinking of those who profit from human trafficking or slave labor; do you think these traffickers and slavers have love for God in their hearts? No, they don't fear the Lord and they are not happy. They are not. I am also thinking of those who manufacture weapons for fomenting wars; just think about what kind of job this is. I am certain that if I were to ask: How many of you manufacture weapons? There would be no one. Weapons manufacturers don't come to hear the Word of God! These people manufacture death, they are merchants of death and they make death into a piece of merchandise. May fear of the Lord make them understand that all things end and one day they will have to answer to God.

General Audience, June 11, 2014

HE KNOWS BETTER
THAN WE DO . . .

—

We ask the Lord for life, health, love, happiness . . . and it is right to do so, but we have to remember that God can bring life from death, which is to say we can experience peace even in sickness, calm even in solitude, and joy even in tears. It is not for us to teach God what to do, to tell Him what we need. He knows better than we do, and we must have faith, because His ways and His thoughts are different from ours.

General Audience, January 25, 2017

MOTHER YEAST AND
THE MOLDY GOSPEL

—

When there were no refrigerators to preserve the **mother yeast** of bread, people gave a small amount of their own leavened dough to a neighbor, and when they needed to make bread again they received a handful of leavened dough back from that woman or from someone else who had received it in her turn. This is reciprocity. Communion is not only the **sharing** but also the **multiplying** of goods, the creation of new bread, of new goods, of new Good with a capital **G**. The principles of the Gospel remain active only if we give them to others—they are love, and love is active when we love, not when we write novels or when we watch soap operas. If, instead, we hoard the Gospel, keep it all to ourselves, these principles get moldy and die. The Gospel can grow moldy. The communion economy will have a future if you share with everyone, if you don't keep the Gospel in your "house" alone. Give the Gospel to everyone, first to the poor and young, who need it most and know how to make your gift bear fruit! To truly live one must learn to give: not just profits, but also of yourselves. The most important gift an entrepreneur can give is himself or herself: money, though important, means too little.

Address, February 4, 2017

BE A MISSIONARY OF JOY EVEN IN TIMES OF STRESS

Saint Paul, in his letter to the Thessalonians, describes what it takes to be "missionaries of joy." We need to pray constantly, always give thanks to God, listen to His Spirit, seek out good, and avoid evil (1 Thessalonians 5:17–22). If this becomes our lifestyle, then the Good News will be able to enter many homes and help people and families rediscover that salvation lies in Jesus. In Him it is possible to find inner peace and the strength to face life every day, even at its heaviest and most difficult. No one has ever heard of a sad saint with a mournful face. This is unheard of! It would be a contradiction. A Christian's heart is filled with peace, because he knows how to place his joy in the Lord even when going through difficult times. To have faith does not mean you never have difficult moments; it means you have the strength to face those moments because you know that you are not alone. This is the peace that God gives to His children.

Angelus, December 14, 2014

From Errors to Forgiveness

It's a good thing to have a
dialogue with your mistakes,
because they teach you.
MEETING WITH YOUNG PEOPLE,
MARCH 31, 2014

HOW DO YOU WANT TO BE SAVED?

How do I want to be saved? In my
way? In some spiritual way, which is
fine, which is good for me, but which
is fixed, clear-cut, and risk-free? Or in
a divine way, which is to say on Jesus's
path, which is always surprising, but
which always opens the doors to the
mystery of the omnipotence of God,
which is the mercy of forgiveness?

Homily at Casa Santa Marta,
October 3, 2014

I learn from my mistakes

I made a mistake, I make mistakes . . . In the Bible, in the Book of Knowledge, they say that the man who is right makes seven mistakes a day . . . So everyone makes mistakes . . . They say that man is the only animal that can fall twice in the same spot, because he does not immediately learn from his mistakes. You might say "I didn't make a mistake," but that won't make you better. It will lead you to vanity, arrogance, pride . . . I think that the mistakes I have made in my life have been and are my greatest teachers. Mistakes teach you so much. They humble you, too, because you can feel like a superman, or superwoman, and then you make a mistake, and this humbles you and puts you in your place. I wouldn't say that I learned from all my mistakes: No, I didn't learn from some of my mistakes because I am stubborn, and it is not easy to learn.

But I learned from a great many of my mistakes, and this has done me much good. Even acknowledging your mistakes is important: I'm wrong here, I'm wrong there, I'm wrong here . . . We just have to be careful not to repeat the same mistake, not to return to the same well . . .

Meeting with Young People,
March 31, 2014

JESUS FORGIVES WITH A CARESS

God forgives not with a command but with a caress. Jesus goes beyond the law and pardons by caressing the wounds of our sins. How many of us deserve punishment! It would be just. But He forgives us! How? Mercy doesn't erase the sin: The forgiveness of God erases sin. Mercy goes beyond that.

Mercy is like the sky above us: We look at the night sky with all its stars, but when the sun comes up, we can't see the stars. This is the mercy of God: a great light of love, of tenderness.

God forgives not with a command but with a caress, caressing the wounds of sin because he is committed to forgiveness, he is committed to our salvation.

Jesus is our confessor. He does not humiliate the adulteress, He does not say to her: What did you do, when did you do it, how did you do it, and whom did you do it with? He tells her to go and sin no more. The mercy of God is great, the mercy of Jesus is great: They forgive us with a caress.

Homily at Casa Santa Marta,
April 7, 2014

FAITH DOES NOT ERADICATE THE BAD, BUT IT OFFERS THE KEY TO GOODNESS

—

Illness, above all serious illness, creates crises and raises deep questions. Our first response may be rebellion: Why has this happened to me? We may feel desperate and think that all is lost, that nothing makes sense ... Our faith in God may be tested, but the power of faith is also revealed. Not because faith makes illness, pain, or our deep questions disappear, but because it offers a key to discovering meaning and purpose, a key that helps us see how illness can bring us closer to Jesus, who walks at our side, weighed down by the Cross.

Message for World Day of the Sick, 2016

JOY FOR THE ADULTERER AND THE SINNER

What joy welled up in the heart of the adulteress (John 8) and the sinner (Luke 7:36–50)! Forgiveness made them feel free and happy as nothing else had. Their tears of shame and pain turned into the smile of a person who knows that he or she is loved. Mercy creates **joy,** because our hearts open up to the hope of a new life. The joy of forgiveness is unmistakable, it radiates all around us whenever we experience it. Its source is God's love as He comes to meet us, breaking down the walls of selfishness that surround us and turning us into instruments of mercy.

Misericordia et Misera 3

ARISE, TAKE HEART!

Isaiah, prophesying today's joy in Jerusalem said this: "Arise, shine." At the start of each day we should welcome this invitation: **Arise, shine**. Follow the bright star of Jesus. If we follow Jesus, we will experience the joy that the Magi felt who "were overjoyed at seeing the star" (Matthew 2:10). **Where there is God, there is joy**. Those who have encountered Jesus have experienced the miracle of light that pierces the darkness, and they know how this light enlightens and illuminates. I would like to invite everyone not to fear this light and to open up to the Lord. Above all, I would like to tell those who have lost their strength to look for the Lord; to those who are tired, to those who feel overwhelmed by the darkness of life and who have extinguished their yearning for God: Arise, take heart! The light of Jesus can overcome the deepest darkness. Arise, take heart!

Angelus, January 6, 2017

BETTER RED THAN YELLOW

We must never tire of asking for forgiveness. You may feel ashamed to tell your sins, but as our mothers and our grandmothers used to say, it is better to be red once than yellow a thousand times. We blush once, but then our sins are forgiven and we go forward.

General Audience, November 20, 2013

WHEN DOES JESUS CRY?

—

Jesus wept when He saw how people resisted Him, and He weeps when He sees our resistance. He wept in front of Lazarus's tomb; He wept while looking at Jerusalem, saying, "But you who kill prophets and stone those who have been sent to you, how many times I wanted to gather your sons as the mother hen gathers her chicks under her wings!" He also weeps at the tragedy when people do not accept the salvation their Father wants for them.

Homily at Casa Santa Marta,
October 3, 2014

WE ALL MAKE MISTAKES, WE CAN ALL CHANGE

—

We all make mistakes: every one of us. In one way or another we have all made a mistake. But hypocrisy causes us to overlook the possibility that other people can change their lives; we have little faith in rehabilitation, reintegration into society. We forget that we are all sinners, and that often, without being aware of it, we, too, are prisoners. We are prisoners when we cling to our prejudices or are slaves to the idols of false comforts. We are prisoners when we adhere too closely to the schemata of an ideology or consider the laws of the markets as absolutes, even as they crush other people. At such times, we imprison ourselves behind the walls of individualism and self-sufficiency, deprived of the truth that sets us free. Pointing the finger at someone else's mistakes cannot excuse concealing our own contradictions.

We know that in God's eyes no one can consider himself righteous (Romans 2:1–11). But no one can live without the certainty of finding forgiveness!

Homily, November 6, 2016

Don't walk in the darkness of self-deception

What does "walking in the dark" mean? We all have darkness in our lives, moments when everything, even our conscience, is dark, no? Going into darkness means being satisfied with yourself. Being convinced that you do not need to be saved. That is darkness! And when one goes down the path of darkness, it is not easy to turn back. Perhaps this is why John reflects, perhaps this is why he says: "If we say, 'We are without sin,' we deceive ourselves and the truth is not in us" (1 John 1:5–22). Look at your sins, at our sins: We are all sinners. All of us. This is the starting point.

But if we confess our sins, He is faithful to us, He is fair enough to pardon our sins and purify us, washing away every iniquity . . . When the Lord forgives us, He is just. Yes, He does what is just, because He came to save us, and when He forgives, He does justice to Himself. "I am your Savior," and thus He welcomes us . . .

"As a father has compassion on his children, so the Lord has compassion on those who fear Him" (Psalm 103:13), toward those who come to Him. This is the tenderness of the Lord. He always understands us, but He also doesn't let us talk: He knows everything. "Stay calm, go in peace," that peace that only He can give.

Homily at Casa Santa Marta,
April 29, 2013

THE REAL BATTLEFIELD IS YOUR HEART

Jesus lived in violent times. Yet He taught that the true battlefield, where violence and peace meet, is the human heart. "From within people, from their hearts, come evil thoughts" (Mark 7:21).

In this context, Christ's message seems radically positive. He tirelessly preached God's unconditional love, which welcomes and forgives. He taught His disciples to love their enemies and to turn the other cheek (Matthew 5:39). When He stopped people from stoning the adulteress (John 8:1–11), and when, on the night before He died, He told Peter to put away his sword (Matthew 26:52), Jesus traced a path of nonviolence. He walked that path to the very end, to the Cross, whereupon He became our peace and destroyed enmity.

Whoever accepts the Good News of Jesus can recognize the violence within and can be healed by God's mercy, thus becoming an instrument of reconciliation. In the words of Saint Francis of Assisi: "As you announce peace with your mouth, make sure that you have greater peace in your heart."

Message for World Day of Peace, 2017

STILL WATER GOES BAD

—

We all know that when water doesn't flow, it goes bad. There is a saying in Spanish, "Still water is the first to corrupt." Don't stay still. We need to walk, take a step every day, with the help of the Lord. God is our Father, He is mercy, He always loves us . . . God has a good memory, He does not forget. God does not forget about us, He always remembers. There is a passage in the Bible by the prophet Isaiah that says: Even if a mother were to forget her child—and that's impossible—I will never forget you (Isaiah 49:15). And this is true: God thinks of me, He remembers me. I am in God's memory.

Address, July 5, 2014

THE UNHAPPINESS
OF THE VINDICTIVE
—

If we live according to the law of "an eye for an eye, a tooth for a tooth," we will never escape the spiral of evil. The Evil One is clever and tricks us into thinking that human justice can save us and save the world! But only the justice of God can save us! The justice of God was revealed on the Cross: The Cross is the judgment of God over all of us and this world. But how does God judge us? By giving His life for us! Here is the supreme act of justice that defeated the prince of this world once and for all; and this supreme act of justice is the supreme act of mercy. Jesus calls us all to follow this path: "Be merciful, just as your Father is merciful" (Luke 6:36). I now ask of you one thing. In silence, let's all think . . . everyone think of a person whom we are annoyed with, or angry with: someone we do not like. Let us think of that person and in silence, at this moment, let us pray for this person and think merciful thoughts.

Angelus, September 15, 2013

OUR ENEMIES ARE HUMAN, TOO

"Love your enemies, and pray for those who persecute you" (Matthew 5:44). This is not easy. These words should not be seen as approval of evil carried out by an enemy, but as an invitation to a loftier outlook, a magnanimous attitude, similar to that of the Heavenly Father, who, Jesus says, "makes His sun rise on the bad and on the good, and causes rain to fall on the just and on the unjust" (verse 45). Even an enemy is also a human being, created in God's image—even if this image is blurred by this person's shameful behavior.

When we speak of "enemies," we should not think about people who are different or removed from us; we should also talk about ourselves, because we may squabble with our neighbor, or with our relatives. So much animosity exists within families—so much! Think about this. Enemies are also those who speak ill of us, who defame us and do us harm. It is not easy to accept that. But we are called to respond to each of them with kindness, with strategies inspired by love.

Angelus, February 19, 2017

HAVE COURAGE, AND ENTER THROUGH THE NARROW DOOR!

Take heart, have the courage to walk through His doorway. Everyone is invited to cross the threshold of faith, to enter His life and have Him enter our life, so that He may transform it, renew it, and give it full and lasting joy.

Over the course of a day we pass many doors, each one of them inviting us in and promising us happiness. But this happiness lasts only for an instant; it exhausts itself and has no future. So I ask you: Which door do we want to go through? And whom do we want to cross the threshold of our life? I say this: Don't be afraid to cross the threshold of faith in Jesus, to let Him enter our lives more and more, to step out of our selfishness, our indifference to others. Jesus can illuminate our life with a light that never goes out. These are not fireworks, this is not a flash of light! No, it is a peaceful light that lasts forever and gives us peace. So is the light we encounter if we enter through Jesus's door. It is true, Jesus's door is a small door, a narrow door, but not because it leads to a torture chamber. It's narrow because He wants us to open our hearts to Him, to recognize ourselves as sinners in need of His salvation, His forgiveness, and His love. We need humility in order to accept His mercy and be renewed by Him.

Angelus, August 25, 2013

DON'T SCOLD OTHERS, SHOW THEM THEIR VALUE

—

Sometimes we try to correct or convert a sinner by scolding him, by pointing out his mistakes and unrighteous behavior. Jesus's attitude toward Zacchaeus shows us another way: We can show those who err their value, the value that God continues to see in spite of everything, despite all their mistakes. These people may feel surprised and happy, which melts hearts and encourages people to bring out the best in themselves.

Giving people confidence makes them grow and change. This is how God acts with us: He does not dwell on our sin, but overcomes it with love and makes us long for goodness. We have all felt longing or regret after making a mistake. And this is what God our Father does, this is what Jesus does. Everyone has some good qualities, and God looks at these in order to draw that person away from evil.

Angelus, October 30, 2016

EACH ONE OF US CARRIES THE RICHNESS AND BURDENS OF OUR PERSONAL HISTORY

We mustn't forget that each one of us carries the richness and the burdens of our personal history; this is what distinguishes us from everyone else.

Our lives, with their joys and sorrows, are unique and unrepeatable. They flow under the merciful gaze of God. This uniqueness requires—particularly of priests—a careful, profound, and farsighted spiritual discernment. Everyone—no matter who they are or where they are in life—should feel accepted by God, should feel that they can actively participate in community life. Anyone can be one of the people of God who journey tirelessly toward the fullness of His Kingdom of justice, love, forgiveness, and mercy.

Misericordia et Misera 14

WHAT DOES THE ROAD TO YOUR SALVATION LOOK LIKE?

—

What do I think my road to salvation looks like? Will it be with Jesus or someone else? Am I free to accept salvation, or am I confusing freedom with autonomy and asking for the salvation that I think seems right? Do I believe that Jesus is the teacher of salvation, or am I seeking and paying gurus to teach me another way? Am I going to choose the right path, or am I going to find refuge in rules and commandments written by men? Is this what makes me feel safe? Can this sense of security—if this is the right way to say this—buy the salvation that Jesus gives us freely, the salvation that is a gift from God?

Homily at Casa Santa Marta,
October 3, 2014

BE BRAVE, GO TO CONFESSION!

It is healthy to feel a little shame. In my country, when a person feels no shame, we say that he is **sinvergüenza**, shameless. But shame can do us good, it makes us more humble. In Confession, a priest receives our shame with love and tenderness and he forgives us on God's behalf. Even from a human point of view, it is good to talk with a brother and vent, to tell the priest what weighs so heavily on your heart. You feel as though you are unburdening yourself before God, with the Church, to your brother. Do not be afraid of Confession! When you are in line to go to Confession, you feel all these things, even shame, but then when you finish Confession, you feel free, grand, beautiful, forgiven, candid, happy. This is the beauty of Confession! I would like to ask you—don't say anything, answer in your heart—when was the last time you went to Confession? Everyone think about it . . . Was it two days ago? Two weeks, two years, twenty years, forty years? Everyone count, everyone ask yourselves, "When was the last time I went to Confession?" And if a lot of time has passed, don't waste another day. Go. The priest will be benevolent. Jesus is there, and Jesus is more benevolent than priests, Jesus receives you, He receives you with so much love. Be brave and go to Confession!

General Audience, February 19, 2014

THE FLOCK AND THE WOLF

—

Jesus leaves an unjust trial and a cruel interrogation, looks into Peter's eyes, and Peter weeps. We ask that He look at us, too, that we allow ourselves to be looked upon. We ask to weep. We ask for the grace of shame so that we can reply, as Peter did, after forty days, "You know that I love You." So that we can hear You say, "Go back on your path, and tend to My sheep." I would add to this, "And don't let any wolves enter the flock."

Homily at Casa Santa Marta, July 7, 2014

A Hundred Eternities

A Christian never loses peace
when he is a real Christian.
HOMILY, DECEMBER 14, 2014

I AM AFRAID OF SEEING DEATH APPROACH

—

Each time we face our death, or the death of a loved one, our faith is put to the test. All our doubts and frailties come to the surface. We wonder, "Will there truly be life after death? Will I still be able to see and embrace the people I have loved?"

Several days ago a woman in an audience asked me, "Will I meet my loved ones?" Her doubt was evident. We need to return to the root and foundation of our faith, so that we can be aware of what God did for us in Jesus Christ and what our death means. We all feel fear on account of this uncertainty about death. It reminds me of an elderly man, a kind old man, who said: "I am not afraid of death. I am afraid of seeing it approach." That's what he was afraid of.

General Audience, February 1, 2017

We inherit big dreams

Simeon's Canticle is the hymn of the believer who at the end of his days can exclaim: "Hope does not disappoint" (Romans 5:5). God never deceives us. Simeon and Anna, in their old age, were capable of a new fruitfulness, and they testify to this in song. Life deserves to be lived in hope, because the Lord keeps His promise. Jesus Himself will later explain this promise in the synagogue of Nazareth: The sick, prisoners, the lonely, the poor, the elderly, and the sinners, all are invited to take up this same hymn of hope. Jesus is with them, and Jesus is with us (Luke 4:18–19).

We inherited this hymn of hope from our elders. They introduced us to this "dynamic." In their faces, in their lives, in their daily and constant sacrifice we were able to see this praise made flesh. We inherit the dreams of our fathers, we inherit the hope that did not disappoint our mothers and forefathers, our older siblings. We are the heirs of those who have gone before us and who had the courage to dream. Like them, we, too, want to sing, "God does not deceive; hope in Him does not disappoint." God comes to meet His people.

Homily, February 2, 2017

The challenge of
the last step

—

The moment of death. The Church has always experienced this dramatic passage in the light of Christ's Resurrection, which opened the way to the certainty of life to come. Death is a true challenge to face, especially in contemporary culture, which often tends to trivialize death, to treat it like a fiction or hide it. Yet we must face death, and prepare for it as a painful and inevitable passage: a passage charged with immense meaning. Death is the ultimate act of love toward those we leave behind and toward God, whom we go to meet. In all religions, the moment of death, like that of birth, is accompanied by a religious presence. As Christians, we celebrate the funeral Liturgy as a hope-filled prayer for the soul of the deceased and as a consolation to those who have suffered the loss of their loved one.

Misericordia et Misera 15

WE WILL ALL HAVE A SUNSET. WHAT WILL YOURS BE LIKE?

—

Hope is like yeast in that it expands to fill your heart and soul. We all have difficult moments in life, but hope helps the soul move forward and see what awaits it. Today is a day of hope. Our brothers and sisters are in the presence of God, and we, too, will be there, in the pure grace of the Lord, if we walk down the path of Jesus. The Apostle John says: "Everyone who has this hope based on Him makes himself pure, as He is pure" (1 John 3:3). Hope cleanses, it makes us lighter; this purification and our hope in Jesus Christ make us hurry. In this pre-sunset of today, we should all think about the sunset of our life: "What will my sunset be like?"

All of us will have a sunset, all of us! Do I envision it with hope? Do I see it with the joy of the Lord's welcome? This is a Christian thought that brings us peace. Today is a day of joy, but a serene, tranquil joy, the joy of peace. Let us think of the sunset of the brothers and sisters who have preceded us, and let us think of our own sunset. And let us think about our heart and ask ourselves: "Where is my heart anchored?" If it is not well anchored, let us drop anchor, here, along these shores, knowing that hope won't let us down because the Lord Jesus doesn't let us down.

Homily, November 1, 2015

WARNING! YOU CAN BRING NEITHER POWER NOR PRIDE TO ETERNITY

—

When a person lives in evil, blasphemes, exploits and tyrannizes others, or lives only for money, vanity, power, or pride, the holy fear of God warns us: Be careful! With all this power, money, pride, and vanity, you will not be happy. You can't take it with you to the other side: There is no money, power, vanity, or pride there. Nothing like that! We can only bring the love that God the Father gives us, God's embrace, which we accept and receive with love. And we can bring what we have done for others. Be careful not to place your hope in money, pride, power, or vanity, because they bring you nothing good!

General Audience, June 11, 2014

VANITY OF VANITIES

—

"Vanity of vanities! All things are vanity!" (Ecclesiastes 1:2). Young people are particularly vulnerable to the empty, meaningless values that often surround them. Unfortunately, they are also the ones who pay the consequences. On the other hand, an encounter with the living Christ and His great family that is the Church fills hearts with joy and true life. Christ fills the heart with a profound goodness that endures and does not change. We can see it on the faces of young people in Rio. But this experience must confront vanity, that poisonous emptiness that creeps into our profit-based and avaricious society. It must confront the consumerism that deceives young people. This Sunday's Gospel reminds us how absurd it is to base our happiness on possessions. The rich say to themselves: My goodness, I have many possessions . . . relax, eat, drink, and be merry! But God says to them: You fool! This very night your life will be demanded of you. And all the things you have accumulated, whose will they be (Luke 12:19–20)? Dear brothers and sisters, the true treasure is the love of God shared with our brethren. That love comes from God and enables us to share it with one another and to help one another. Those who experience it do not fear death and their hearts are at peace.

Angelus, August 4, 2013

What is the Kingdom of Heaven?

—

What is the **Kingdom of God**, and what is the **Kingdom of Heaven**? They are the same thing. They both make us think of the afterlife: eternal life. Of course, the Kingdom of God will stretch far beyond earthly life, but the Good News that Jesus brings us—and that John proclaims—is that we do not need to wait for the future Kingdom of God: It is here now. Since it is already here, we can experience its spiritual influence. "The Kingdom of God is in your midst!" Jesus would say. God rules over our history, today, every day of our lives; and where His rule is welcomed with faith and humility, love, joy, and peace will blossom.

Angelus, December 4, 2016

WE WILL BE LIKE ANGELS

This life is lived with temporary realities—and they will end. In the afterlife, after our resurrection, death will no longer be our horizon. Everything, even human relationships, will be transfigured by God. Even marriage, a sign and instrument of God in this world, will shine brightly, transformed in the full light of the glorious communion of saints in Paradise.

The "sons of Heaven and of the Resurrection" are not a privileged few but all men and women, because Jesus brings salvation for all of us. And the life of the risen will be like that of angels (Luke 20:36), that is, wholly immersed in the light of God, completely devoted to His praise, in an eternity filled with joy and peace. But remember! Resurrection is not only about rising from the dead, it is a way of life that we can experience now. Resurrection is a victory over nothingness, a victory that we anticipate now. Resurrection is the foundation of faith and of Christian hope!

Angelus, November 6, 2016

Your fulfillment will be in God

—

Job was in darkness. He was right at death's door. And at that moment of anguish, pain, and suffering, Job proclaimed hope: "I know that my Vindicator lives, and that He will at last stand forth upon the dust . . . My own eyes, not another's, will behold Him" (19:25, 27). A cemetery is sad, because it reminds us of our loved ones who have passed on. It also makes us think of our future, of our own death. But in this sadness, we bring flowers, as a sign of hope, and also, I might say, of celebration. But for later on, not now. Our sorrow and our hope mingle. We feel sorrow at the memory of our loved ones, before their remains, and also hope. Our hope helps us, because we, too, must make this journey. Everyone will make this journey. Sooner or later, with or without pain, everyone will make this journey. But there is always that flower of hope, that powerful thread that is anchored in the hereafter: the hope of resurrection. Jesus was the first to make this journey. We are following the journey that He made . . . "I know that my Vindicator lives, and that He will at last stand forth upon the dust . . . I will see for myself, my own eyes, not another's, will behold Him."

Homily, November 2, 2016

BE A SAINT, WHEREVER YOU ARE!

—

Some people think that holiness is a matter of closing your eyes and looking like a saintly icon. No! This is not true holiness! Holiness is something greater and deeper, something God gives us. We become holy by living with love and offering our own Christian witness in everyday life, in the circumstances and lives in which we find ourselves.

Are you consecrated?

Be holy by living out your gift and your ministry with joy.

Are you married?

Be holy by loving and taking care of your husband or your wife, as Christ did for the Church.

If you are unmarried but baptized?

Be holy by carrying out your work honestly and skillfully and by helping others.

"But, Father, I work in a factory; I

work as an accountant, only with numbers; you can't be a saint there . . ."

"Yes, yes, you can! You can become a saint wherever you are. God gives you the grace to become holy. God reaches out to you." Always, anywhere, one can become holy. You can open yourself up to the grace that lives inside us and leads us to holiness.

Are you a parent or a grandparent?

Be a saint by teaching your children or grandchildren to know and follow Jesus. It takes a lot of patience to do this. Being a good parent, a good grandfather, a good mother, a good grandmother takes patience, and through this patience comes holiness. Holiness comes by exercising patience.

Are you a Sunday school teacher, an educator, or a volunteer?

Be holy by becoming a visible sign of God's love and of His presence among us.

There you have it: Every state of life can lead to holiness! Your everyday life can lead you to holiness. The path to sainthood is open in your home, on the road, and at work, as well as in church. Don't be scared of following this path. It is God who gives us grace. The Lord asks only this: that we be in communion with Him and that we serve our brothers and sisters.

General Audience, November 19, 2014

WHO DOESN'T BELIEVE IN RESURRECTION?

—

Unfortunately, many have often tried to cloud our faith in the Resurrection of Jesus. Doubts creep in, even among believers. We call this a "rosewater" faith, it is watered down—it's not a strong faith. This "rosewater" faith is a result of superficiality and indifference: Either we are busy with a thousand things we think more important than faith, or we are wearing blinders. But it is the Resurrection itself that brings hope, for it opens our life and the entire world to the eternal future of God, to full happiness, to the certainty that evil, sin, and death can be overcome. And this helps us trust, which helps us face our everyday lives with courage and determination. Christ's Resurrection illuminates everyday life with a new light. The Resurrection of Christ is our strength!

General Audience, April 3, 2013

WALK TOWARD THE DOOR!

Christian hope is a shield. When we talk about hope we often think of the common meaning of the term, as something beautiful that we want but that may or may not be attained. We "hope" something will happen; it is like a wish. People say, for example, "I hope we have good weather tomorrow!" But we know that there might be bad weather . . . Christian hope is not like this. Christian hope is the expectation of something that has already been fulfilled: The door is there and I hope to reach the door. So what should I do? Walk toward the door! I am certain that I will reach it. This is Christian hope: the certainty that I am walking toward something, not just the wish for it.

General Audience, February 1, 2017

WE WILL ALL BE UP THERE TOGETHER

—

We know, from the book of Revelation, that God is preparing a new home and a new earth for justice, a place where happiness will fill our hearts with peace. This is the Church's mission. As the Bible says, this is the "new Jerusalem" and "Paradise." More than a place, Paradise is a state of being in which our deepest hopes are fulfilled and in which we, as creatures and children of God, reach our full maturity. We will finally be clothed in the joy, peace, and love of God, completely, without limit, and we will come face to face with Him! It is beautiful to think of this, to think of Heaven. We will all be there together. It is beautiful, it gives strength to the soul.

General Audience, November 26, 2014

THE SLOWNESS OF THE KINGDOM

Choosing God and His Kingdom does not always immediately bear fruit. It is a hopeful decision, a decision whose realization is left up to God. Christian hope focuses on the future, on God's fulfillment of His promise. We do not stop hoping in the face of difficulty, because Christian hope is based on God's fidelity, which is eternal. God is true, He is a faithful father, a faithful friend, and a loyal ally.

Angelus, February 26, 2017

ONLY THE POOR
REALLY KNOW HOPE

—

When a woman realizes she is pregnant, every day is filled with waiting, waiting to see her child for the first time. This is how we should live, in the expectation of seeing the Lord, of encountering the Lord. It is not easy, but you can learn to live with anticipation. To hope means to have a humble heart, a poor heart. Only a poor man truly knows how to wait. A man who is full of himself, full of his achievements and his possessions, does not know how to place his trust in anyone other than himself.

General Audience, February 1, 2017

DON'T LET THE LAMP OF HOPE
BURN OUT

—

Christian hope is more than a wish. It is not optimism. For a Christian, hope is fervent expectation. It is waiting ardently for the ultimate and definitive fulfillment of a mystery: the mystery of God's love, in which we are reborn and which we are already living.

It is waiting for someone who is about to arrive: Christ the Lord approaches ever closer, day by day, and He will bring us into the fullness of His communion and of His peace.

The Church has the task of keeping the lamp of hope burning brightly, so that it may continue to shine as a sure sign of salvation for all humanity, so that it can illuminate the path that leads to an encounter with all-merciful God.

General Audience, October 15, 2014

BE A SIGN THAT ANTICIPATES THE JOYS OF HEAVEN

—

The firm certainty of God's love lies at the heart of religious vocation. Become a tangible sign of the presence of God's

Kingdom for others, a hint of the eternal joys of Heaven. If our testimony is joyful, we will attract men and women to Christ. Prayer, meditating on the Word of God, and celebrating the Sacraments and life in community nourish joy, which is very important.

When these are lacking, weaknesses and difficulties will emerge and dampen the joy we knew so well at the beginning of our journey.

Address, August 16, 2014

YOU ARE IN HIS HANDS

—

We must firmly believe that the Lord does not abandon us; we need to walk in hope and work to build a better world, despite any difficulties and troubles that mark our personal and collective lives. This is how the Christian community is called to encounter the "day of the Lord" . . .

In the Gospel, Jesus urges us to affix this belief in our minds and hearts, to be certain that God guides our history and that He knows how everything will end. Under the Lord's merciful gaze, history unfurls and weaves between good and evil. All that happens is contained within Him: Our lives are in His hands.

Angelus, November 13, 2016

A CHRISTIAN MAKES NO DISTINCTION BETWEEN WHO IS DEAD AND WHO IS NOT, ONLY BETWEEN WHO IS IN CHRIST AND WHO IS NOT

—

It is good to understand the kind of continuity and deep communion that exists between the Church in Heaven and the one on earth. Those who already live in the presence of God can sustain us and pray for us. At the same time, we are invited to offer up good works, prayer, and the Eucharist in order to alleviate the suffering of souls who are waiting for the bliss of the Beatitudes. For the Christian, there is no distinction between who is dead and who is alive, only between who is in Christ and who is not! This is what determines our salvation and our happiness.

General Audience, November 26, 2014

WHAT ARE WE WAITING FOR?

The vision of Heaven described in the book of Revelation is truly beautiful: There's the Lord God, beauty, goodness, truth, tenderness, and love in its fullness. All of this awaits us. Those who have gone before us and who have died in the Lord are there. They proclaim that they have been saved not through their own works—though they surely did good works—but that they have been saved by the Lord: "Salvation comes from our God, who is seated on the throne, and from the Lamb!" (7:10).

It is He who saves us, it is He who at the end of our lives takes us by the hand like a father and accompanies us to that Heaven where our ancestors are. One of the elders asks: "Who are these wearing white robes, and where did they come from?" (verse 13).

Who are these righteous ones, these saints who are in Heaven? The answer: "These are the ones who have survived the time of great distress; they have washed their robes and made them white in the blood of the Lamb" (verse 14). We can enter Heaven only thanks to the blood of the Lamb, thanks to the blood of Christ. Christ's own blood has redeemed us, which has opened the gates of Heaven to us. And if today we remember our brothers and sisters who have gone before us in life and are in Heaven, it is because they have been washed in the blood of Christ.

This is our hope: the hope of Christ's blood! It is a hope that does not disappoint. If we walk with the Lord in life, He will never disappoint us!

Homily, November 1, 2015

WE'RE WAITING FOR THE GROOM!

—

We are waiting for Jesus's return! The Church, as bride, awaits her groom! We must ask ourselves, however, with total sincerity: Are we truly luminous and credible witnesses of this expectation, of this hope? Do our communities still live in the sign of the presence of the Lord Jesus and in the fervent expectation of His coming? Or do they appear tired, sluggish, weighed down by fatigue and resignation? Do we run

the risk of exhausting the oil of faith,
the oil of joy? Let's be careful!
General Audience, October 15, 2014

EVERY ACTION IS A SEED THAT BLOSSOMS IN THE GARDEN OF GOD

—

If there were no references to Paradise
and to eternal life, Christianity would
be reduced to ethics, to a philosophy of
life. Instead, the message of Christian
faith comes from Heaven, it is revealed
by God and goes beyond this world.
Belief in the Resurrection is essential,
so that each act of Christian love is not
ephemeral, not an end in itself, but a
seed destined to blossom in the garden
of God, and to produce the fruit of
eternal life.

May the Virgin Mary, Queen of
Heaven and Earth, strengthen our
hope of resurrection and help us per-

form good works, thereby making Her Son's word, which has been sown in our hearts, fruitful.

Angelus, November 6, 2016

EVERYTHING IS TRANSFORMED, AND YOU WILL HAVE JOY

—

Everything changes: The desert blooms, comfort and joy suffuse our hearts. These signs are fulfilled in Jesus. He Himself affirms them by responding to the messengers sent by John the Baptist—what does Jesus say to these messengers? "The blind regain their sight, the lame walk, lepers are cleansed, the deaf hear, the dead are raised up" (Matthew 11:5).

These are more than words, they are facts that demonstrate how salvation, brought by Jesus, grabs us and regenerates us. God entered history in order to free us from the slavery of sin; He set up His tent in our midst to share our lives, to heal and bind our wounds, and to give us new life. Joy is the fruit of this salvation, the fruit of God's love.

God wants us to be drawn in by the feeling of exultation. By exultation, by joy ... A Christian who isn't joyful is a Christian who is lacking something, or else they are not a Christian! Heartfelt joy, the joy within us, leads us forward and gives us courage. The Lord comes, He comes into our life as a liberator; He comes to free us from all forms of slavery; He shows us the way of loyalty, of patience, and of perseverance. When He returns, our joy will know no bounds.

Angelus, December 11, 2016

THE "RULE OF LIFE" OF A BELIEVER WHO LONGS FOR GOD

—

A holy longing for God wells up in the hearts of believers, because they know that the Gospel is not of the past but of the present. A holy longing for God keeps us alert in the face of every attempt to weaken and impoverish our life. A holy longing for God is the memory of faith, which rebels before all prophets of doom. That longing keeps hope alive in the believers, who from week to week continue to plead: "Come, Lord Jesus."

This same longing led the elderly Simeon to go to the Temple every day, certain that his life would not end before he held the Savior in his arms. This longing led the prodigal son to abandon his self-destructive lifestyle and to seek his father's embrace. This longing led the shepherd to leave the ninety-nine sheep in order to find the one that was lost. Mary Magdalene experienced this longing on that Sunday morning when she ran to the tomb and met her Risen Master.

Longing for God draws us out of isolation, which makes us think that nothing can change. Longing for God shatters our dreary routines and pushes us to make the changes we want and need. Longing for God has its roots in the past, yet it does not remain there: It reaches out to the future.

The believer who feels this longing is driven by his faith to seek God, as the Magi did, in the most distant corners of history. Like the Magi, the believer knows that the Lord is waiting.

Homily, January 6, 2017

CLING TO THE ANCHOR'S ROPE

In the Second Reading, we learn what the Apostle John said to his disciples: "See what love the Father has bestowed on us, that we may be called the children of God. Yet so we are. The reason the world does not know us . . . We are God's children now; what we shall be has not yet been revealed. We know that when it is revealed, we shall be like Him, for we shall see Him as He is"

(1 John 3:1–2). To see God, to be like God: This is our hope. And today, on All Saints' Day and before the Day of the Dead, we need to think a little about this hope: this hope that accompanies us in life. The first Christians portrayed hope as an anchor, as though life were an anchor cast on Heaven's shores and all of us are journeying to that shore, clinging to the anchor's rope. This is a beautiful image of hope: to imagine our hearts anchored where our beloved predecessors are, where the saints are, where Jesus is, where God is. This is the hope that does not disappoint; today and tomorrow are days of hope.

Homily, November 1, 2015

Your only sadness: not being a saint. Your only misery: not being a son

—

Christ's poverty enriches us. He becomes flesh and bears our weaknesses and sins as an expression of God's infinite mercy to us. Christ's poverty is the greatest treasure of all: Jesus is rich in His infinite love in God the Father, His constant trust, His desire always to seek His Father's will and glory. Jesus's wealth is that of a child who loves and is loved by his parents, never doubting their love and tenderness for an instant. Jesus's wealth lies in being **the Son;** His unique relationship with the Father is the sovereign prerogative of this poor Messiah. When Jesus asks us to take up His "yoke, which is easy," He asks us to be enriched by His "poverty, which is rich" and His "richness, which is poor," to share His filial and fraternal

Spirit, to become sons and daughters in the Son, brothers and sisters in the firstborn Brother (Romans 8:29).

The poet Léon Bloy said that true regret lies in not being a saint; we could also say that there is only one real kind of misery: not living as children of God and brothers and sisters of Christ.

Message for Lent, 2014

PART IV

THEY WHO PRAY
LIVE SERENELY

Prayer Completes Us

We need to make room for the Spirit, so that He may counsel us. Making room is praying, praying that He always comes and helps us.

GENERAL AUDIENCE, MAY 7, 2014

WHY POPE FRANCIS IS HAPPY

Q. (**Boy**): Everyone tries to be happy. But we were wondering, are you happy? And why?

A. (**Pope Francis**): Absolutely, absolutely, I am happy. I am happy because . . . I don't know why . . . maybe because I have a job, I am not unemployed, I have a job, a job as shepherd! I am happy because I have found my path in life, and traveling down this path makes me happy. It's a peaceful happiness, because the happiness of my age is not the same as the happiness of youth. There's a certain inner peace, a vast peace, a happiness that comes with age. And although there are always problems along the path—even now there are problems—this happiness doesn't go away. No, this happiness sees the problems, it endures them and then it moves on, it tries to resolve them and then it moves on. But in the depths of my heart there is peace and happiness, because of God's grace, really. It's His grace, not my merit.

Meeting with Young People,
March 31, 2014

THERE ARE AS MANY DIFFERENT WAYS TO PRAY AS THERE ARE PEOPLE

—

There are many different ways to pray for our neighbor! All of them are valid and accepted by God if they come from the heart. I am thinking in particular of the mothers and fathers who bless their children in the morning and the evening. This is still a practice in some families: Blessing a child is a kind of prayer. I'm also thinking of the prayers for the sick, when we visit them and pray for them; of silent intercession, at times tearful, in the many difficult situations that require prayer.

General Audience, November 30, 2016

PRAY WITH YOUR ACTIONS

—

Yesterday a good man, an entrepreneur, came to Mass at Casa Santa Marta. This young man has to close his factory. He wept and said, "I don't want to leave more than fifty families without work. I can declare the company bankrupt: I would go home with my money, but my heart would weep for these fifty families for the rest of my life." This is a good Christian who prays through his actions: He came to Mass to ask the Lord for a solution, not just for himself, but for the fifty families. This is a man who knows how to pray, both with his heart and with his actions. He knows how to pray for his neighbor. He is in a difficult situation. But he doesn't settle for the easy way out: "They'll manage somehow." He is a Christian. Listening to him made me happy! Maybe there are many people like him these days, when so many people are suffering from unemployment.

General Audience, November 30, 2016

THE REAL CHRISTIAN PRAYER
SAYS: FATHER

Jesus says that the Father in Heaven "knows what you need even before you ask for it." **Father.** This is the key to prayer. Without saying this word, without hearing this word, we cannot pray. Whom do I pray to? Almighty God? Too far away. I don't feel close to Him, nor did Jesus. Whom do I pray to? Universal God? That's a little banal these days, no? "Pray to the universal god." This polytheistic formality seems superficial.

We need to pray to "our" Father, the Father who created you, the Father who gave us all life: you, me . . . He accompanies you on your path; He knows your whole life; He knows the good you've done and the not so good, too. He knows everything . . . If we don't begin our prayers with this unspoken

"Father"—said within our hearts—we cannot pray like Christians.

Homily at Casa Santa Marta,
June 20, 2013

LET THE SPIRIT PRAY IN YOU

—

I think about how we can give thanks for good news about a friend, a relative, a coworker . . . "Thank you, Lord, for this wonderful thing!" That, too, is praying for others! Thank the Lord when things go well. At times, as Saint Paul says, "We do not know how to pray as we ought, but the Spirit Itself intercedes with inexpressible groanings" (Romans 8:26). It is the Spirit that prays within us. Therefore, let us open our hearts so that the Holy Spirit can scrutinize our deepest desires, purify them, and bring them to fulfillment. For us and for others, let us always ask that God's will be done, as the **Our Father** says, because His will is the greatest good. It is the goodness of a Father who never abandons us. Pray and let the Holy Spirit pray in us. This makes life beautiful: being able to pray, to give thanks and praise the Lord, to ask for something, to weep when there are difficulties. But let's keep our hearts open to the Spirit so that He may pray in us, with us, and for us.

General Audience, November 30, 2016

PRAY TO THE FATHER
WHO LOVES ALL
—

Is God a Father to me alone? No, He is our Father, because I am not an only son. None of us is. If I cannot be a brother to all, then I will have a hard time becoming a son of this Father—because while He is definitely my Father, He is also the Father to many other people, so they are all my brothers . . . If I am not at peace with my brothers, I can't call Him Father. This is how we explain how Jesus, after teaching us the **Our Father,** says right away, "If you forgive others their sins, your Heavenly Father will forgive you, too; but if you don't forgive others, the Father won't forgive you your sins . . ."

This is difficult, yes, very difficult. It isn't easy. But Jesus promised us the Holy Spirit. It is He who teaches from within, from the heart, teaches us how to say "Our" and "Father"—and this is how He helps us make peace with our enemies.

Homily at Casa Santa Marta,
June 20, 2013

PRAYER MAKES ROOM

We always return to the same theme: prayer! Prayer is so important. It's important to pray with the prayers that we learned as children, but also to pray with our own words. To be able to ask the Lord: "Lord, help me, advise me, what must I do now?" Prayer makes room for the Spirit to come and help us, to teach us what to do. Prayer! Never forget prayer. Never! No one knows when we are praying—we might be on the bus, or walking down the street: we pray in the silence of our heart. Let us take advantage of these moments to pray, pray that the Spirit gives us the gift of counsel.

General Audience, May 7, 2014

LEARN WHAT TO SAY TO THE LORD

—

Jesus teaches us: The Father knows all. Don't worry, the Father sends rain to the righteous and the sinners alike; He sends sun to the just and sun to the sinners. Starting today, I would like everyone to take five minutes out of their day, pick up your Bibles, and slowly recite Psalm 102 . . .

Bless the LORD, O my soul,
And do not forget all His gifts,
Who pardons all your sins,
And heals all your ills,
Who redeems your life from the
    pit,
And crowns you with mercy and
    compassion.

Say it all. Pray. This is how we learn what we have to say to the Lord when we pray for grace.
Homily at Casa Santa Marta, July 1, 2013

NOT WHAT PLEASES ME, BUT WHAT PLEASES HIM

—

When we commune with God and listen to His Word, we gradually set aside our personal logic, which is mostly determined by our limitations, prejudices, and ambitions. We learn to ask the Lord: What is Your wish? What is Your will? What pleases You? This is how a **deep,**

almost connatural, harmony in the Spirit grows and develops within us. We experience the truth of Jesus's words, as written in the Gospel of Matthew: "Do not worry about how you are to speak or what you are to say. You will be given at that moment what you are to say. For it will not be you who speaks, but the Spirit of your Father speaking through you" (10:19–20).

General Audience, May 7, 2014

FAMILIES WHO PRAY TOGETHER

I would like to ask you, dear families: Do you pray together as a family? Some of you do, I know. But so many people ask me: how? Well, we have to be like the tax collector: humble before God. Each one of us needs to humbly look to the Lord and ask for His goodness, for Him to come to us. But how do we do this as a family? After all, prayer is so personal, and it's never the perfect time, there's never a quiet moment in families ... Yes, this is true, but it's also a question of humility, of recognizing that we need God, just like the tax collector! All families need God: all of us! We need His help, His strength, His blessing, His mercy, His forgiveness. And praying as a family is simple enough: It's very simple! Saying the **Our Father** together around the table is not something extraordinary: It's easy. And saying the Rosary together, as a family, is very beautiful. It's a source of great strength! You can also pray for one another: The husband prays for his wife, the wife for her husband, they both pray for their children, the children pray for their parents and their grandparents ... Everyone prays for one another. This is what praying in the family means and this is what makes a family strong: prayer.

Homily, October 22, 2013

Pope Francis's Prayers for a Fulfilling Life

Maybe this sounds bad, but praying is a little like pestering God so that He listens to us.

DECEMBER 6, 2013

CHILD'S PRAYER, TAUGHT BY JESUS

—

Our Father, in Heaven,
Hallowed be Your Name.
Your Kingdom come,
Your will be done,
On earth as in Heaven.
Give us today our daily bread
And forgive us our debts
As we forgive our debtors.
And do not subject us to the final
    test,

But deliver us from the Evil One.
Amen.

THE PSALM OF THE JOY
OF THE FULFILLED MAN
—

(Recited by Pope Francis at the beginning of **Amoris Laetitia**):

Blessed are all who fear the LORD,
And who walk in His ways .

What your hands provide you will
   enjoy;
You will be blessed and prosper.
Your wife will be like a fruitful vine
Within your home,
Your children like young olive
   plants
Around your table.

Just so will the man be blessed
Who fears the LORD.

May the LORD bless you from Zion;
May you see Jerusalem's prosperity
All the days of your life,

And live to see your children's
children.
Peace upon Israel.

Psalms 128:1–6

THE PSALM OF THOSE WHO WANT TO LEARN WHAT TO ASK FROM GOD

—

(Pope Francis invites people to read this slowly every day. See the Homily at Casa Santa Marta from July 1, 2013, "Learn What to Say to the Lord"):

Bless the LORD, my soul;
All my being, bless His holy name!

Bless the LORD, my soul;
And do not forget all His gifts,

Who pardons all your sins,
And heals all your ills,

Who redeems your life from the
    pit,
And crowns you with mercy and
    compassion,

Who fills your days with good
    things,
So your youth is renewed like the
    eagle's.

The LORD does righteous deeds,
Brings justice to all the oppressed.

He made known His ways to Moses,
To the Israelites His deeds.

Merciful and gracious is the LORD,
Slow to anger, abounding in mercy.

He will not always accuse,
And nurses no lasting anger;

He has not dealt with us as our sins
  merit,
Nor requited us as our wrongs
  deserve.

For as the heavens tower over the
  earth,
So His mercy towers over those
  who fear Him;

As far as the east is from the west,
So far has He removed our sins
  from us.

As a father has compassion on his
  children,
So the LORD has compassion on
  those who fear Him.

For He knows how we are formed,
Remembers that we are dust.

As for man, his days are like the
  grass;

He blossoms like a flower in the
   field.

A wind sweeps over it and it is gone;
Its place knows it no more.

But the LORD's mercy is from age
   to age,
Toward those who fear Him,
His salvation is for the children's
   children,

Of those who keep His covenant
And remember to carry out His
   precepts.

The LORD has set His throne in
   Heaven;
His dominion extends over all.

Bless the LORD, all you His angels,
Mighty in strength, acting at His
   behest,
Obedient to His command.

Bless the LORD, all you His hosts,
His ministers, who carry out His
  will.

Bless the LORD, all His creatures,
Everywhere in His domain.
Bless the LORD, my soul.

Psalm 103

PRAYER OF SOMEONE WHO WANTS TO RETURN

—

LORD,
I have let myself be deceived;
In a thousand ways I have shunned
  Your love,
Yet here I am once more
To renew my covenant with You.
I need You.
Save me once again, Lord Jesus,
Take me once more into Your
  redeeming embrace.

Evangelii Gaudium 3

PRAY, MARY, FOR US PILGRIMS IN TIME

—

Thank You, O Holy Mother of the
  Son of God,
Holy Mother of God!
Thank You for Your humility,
  which drew the gaze of God;
Thank You for the faith with which
  You received His Word;
Thank You for the courage with
  which You said "Here I am,"
Forgetting Yourself, enthralled by
  Holy Love,
Made wholly one with His hope.
Thank you, O Holy Mother of
  God!
Pray for us, pilgrims in time;
Help us to walk on the path of
  peace.
Amen.

Angelus, January 1, 2017

Sustain us, Mother, in the trusting expectation of our hearts

—

Mary, our Mother,
In Christ You welcome each of us as
a son or daughter.
Sustain the trusting expectation of
our hearts,
Aid us in our infirmities and
sufferings,
And guide us to Christ, Your Son
and our Brother.
Help us give ourselves to the Father
who accomplishes great things.
Message for World Day of the Sick, 2017

For the happiness of men and women in the religious vocation

—

Father of Mercy,
Who gave Your Son for our
salvation

And who strengthens us always
  with the gifts of Your Spirit,
Grant us Christian communities
  that are alive, fervent and
  joyous,
That are fonts of fraternal life,
And that nurture in the young the
  desire to consecrate themselves
To You and to evangelization.
Sustain these communities in their
  commitment
To offer appropriate vocational
  catechesis
And paths to each one's particular
  consecration.
Grant the wisdom
Needed for vocational discernment,
So that in all things the greatness
Of Your merciful love may shine
  forth.
May Mary, Mother and guide of
  Jesus,
Intercede for each Christian
  community

So that, made fruitful by the Holy
   Spirit,
It may be a source of true vocations
For the service of the holy People of
   God.
Message for the Day of Vocations, 2016

WHEN WE PRESENT OURSELVES TO YOU

—

(Prayer for the deceased by Antonio
Rungi, recited by Pope Francis during
the Angelus):

God of infinite mercy,
We entrust to Your immense
   goodness
All those who have left this world
   for eternity,
Where You wait for all humanity
Redeemed by the precious blood of
   Christ
Your Son, who died as a ransom for
   our sins.

Look not, O LORD, on our poverty,
Our suffering, our human
   weakness,
When we appear before You to be
   judged
For joy or for condemnation.
Look upon us with mercy,
Born from the tenderness of Your
   heart,
And help us walk
On the path toward complete
   purification.
Let none of Your children be lost
In the eternal fire of Hell,
Where there can be no repentance.

We entrust to You, O LORD, the
   souls of our beloved dead,
Of those who have died
Without the comfort of the
   Sacraments,
Or who have not had an
   opportunity to repent,
Even at the end of their lives.

May none of them be afraid to
   meet You
After their earthly pilgrimage,
But may they always hope to be
   welcomed in the embrace
Of Your infinite mercy.

May our sister, corporal death,
   always find us vigilant in prayer
And filled with the goodness
   achieved in the course of our
   short or long lives.
LORD, may no earthly thing ever
   separate us from You,
But may everyone and everything
   support us
With a burning desire to rest
   peacefully
And eternally in You.
Amen.

                Angelus, November 2, 2014

INVOCATION FOR PEACE

Lord God of Peace, hear our prayer!

We have tried so many times and for so many years to resolve our conflicts with our own strength and also with our own weapons. There have been many moments of hostility and darkness; so much bloodshed; so many broken lives; so many buried hopes . . . But our efforts have been in vain.

Now, Lord, help us! Grant us peace, teach us peace; guide us toward peace. Open our eyes and our hearts, and give us the courage to say: "No more war!" and "War destroys everything." Grant us the courage to take concrete steps to achieve peace. Lord, God of Abraham, God of the Prophets, God of Love, You created us and You call us to live as brothers and sisters. Give us the strength to be craftsmen of peace every day; give us the strength to see everyone who crosses our path as our brother or sister. Make us sensitive to the pleas of our citizens who entreat us to turn our weapons of war into instruments of peace, our fear into trust, and our tensions into forgiveness. Keep the flame of hope alive in us so that we consistently and patiently choose dialogue and reconciliation, because only these will ultimately bring peace. May the words "division," "hatred," and "war" be banished from the heart of all men. Lord, disarm our tongues and hands, renew our hearts and minds so that the word that always brings us together will be "brother," so that our way of life will always be that of Shalom, Peace, Salaam!

Amen.

Invocation for Peace, June 8, 2014

For Mary,
woman who listens
—

Mary, woman who listens,
Open our ears;
Grant us to know how to listen to
   the Word
Of Your Son Jesus among the
   thousands of words of this
   world;
Grant that we may listen to the
   reality in which we live,
To every person we encounter,
Especially those who are poor, in
   need, in hardship.

Mary, woman of decision,
Illuminate our minds and our
   hearts,
So that we may obey the Word
Of Your Son Jesus without
   hesitation;
Give us the courage to decide

Not to let ourselves be dragged
   along,
Letting others direct our life.

Mary, woman of action,
Make it so that our hands and feet
Move with haste toward others,
Bringing them the charity and love
   of Your Son Jesus,
Bringing, as You did, the light of
   the Gospel to the world.
Amen.

Homily, May 31, 2013

HOLY THURSDAY PRAYER
FOR PRIESTS

On this Holy Thursday, I ask the Lord
Jesus to help many young people discover the ardor in the heart that kindles
joy as soon as we have the bold audac-
ity to respond promptly to His call.

On this Holy Thursday, I ask the Lord

Jesus to preserve the joy that sparkles in the eyes of the recently ordained who go forth to "devour" the world, to be consumed fully in the midst of God's faithful people, rejoicing as they prepare their first homily, their first Mass, their first Baptism, their first Confession . . . It is the joy of sharing—with awe—for the first time as God's anointed, the treasure of the Gospel, and feeling that the faithful are anointing you in another way: with their requests, by bowing their heads for your blessing, by taking your hands, by bringing you their children, by pleading for their sick . . .

Preserve, LORD,
In Your young priests
The joy of going forth,
Of doing everything as if for the
   first time,
The joy of spending their lives fully
   for You.

On this priestly Thursday, I ask the Lord Jesus to confirm the priestly joy of those who have ministered for several years. The joy that, without leaving their eyes, lies on the shoulders of those who bear the weight of the ministry, those priests who, having experienced the labors of the apostolate, gather their strength and rearm themselves: who "get a second wind," as athletes say.

> Preserve, LORD,
> The depth, wisdom, and maturity
> Of the joy felt by these older
>   priests.
> May they be able to pray like
>   Nehemiah:
> "The joy of the LORD is my
>   strength" (8:10).

Finally, on this Thursday of the priesthood, I ask the Lord Jesus to celebrate the joy of elderly priests, be they sick or healthy. It is the joy of the Cross, which springs from knowing that we possess an imperishable treasure in clay jars that are wasting away. May these priests find happiness wherever they are; may they experience in the fleeting passage of the years a taste of Eternity.*

May they know, LORD,
The joy of passing on the torch,
The joy of seeing the children of
    children grow,
And the joy of welcoming, with a
    smile and at peace,
The promises and the hope that
    never disappoint.

Homily, April 17, 2014

*Pope Francis is referring to the theological work of Romano Guardini, a twentieth-century Catholic priest.

PRAYER TO THE VIRGIN SO THAT SHE TRANSFORMS OUR HEART

—

Mary, Virgin and Mother,
You who, moved by the Holy Spirit,
Welcomed the Word of life
In the depths of Your humble faith,
As You gave Yourself completely to
    the Eternal One,
Help us to say yes
To our own urgent call, as pressing
    as ever,
To proclaim the Good News of
    Jesus.
Filled with Christ's presence,
You brought joy to John the
    Baptist,
Making him exult in the womb of
    his mother.
Brimming with joy,
You sang of the wonders of the
    LORD.
Standing at the foot of the Cross

With unwavering faith,
You received the joyful consolation
   of the Resurrection
And gathered the disciples in
   expectation of the Spirit
So that the evangelizing Church
   might be born.
Obtain for us now a new ardor
   born of the Resurrection,
That we may bring to all the
   Gospel of life
That triumphs over death.
Give us a holy courage to seek new
   paths,
That the gift of unfading beauty
May reach every man and woman.
Virgin of listening and
   contemplation,
Mother of love, Bride of the eternal
   marriage,
Pray for the Church, whose pure
   icon You are,
That she may never be closed in on
   herself

Or lose her passion for establishing
  God's Kingdom.
Star of the new evangelization,
Help us to bear radiant witness to
  communion,
To service, to ardent and generous
  faith,
To justice and to love of the poor,
So that the joy of the Gospel
May reach to the ends of the
  earth,
Illuminating even the fringes of
  our world.
Mother of the living Gospel,
Source of joy for the little ones,
Pray for us.
Amen. Alleluia!

Evangelii Gaudium 288

Saint Faustina's Prayer

—

(Pope Francis invited everyone to recite this in the Message for World Youth Day, 2016):

Help me, O Lord,
That my eyes may be merciful,
So that I may never suspect
Or judge by appearances,
But look for what is beautiful
In my neighbors' souls and come to
   their rescue . . . ;
That my ears may be merciful,
So that I may give heed to my
   neighbors' needs,
And not be indifferent
To their pains and moanings . . . ;
That my tongue may be merciful,
So that I will never speak negatively
   of my neighbor,
But have a word of comfort
And forgiveness for all . . . ;

That my hands may be merciful
and filled with good deeds . . . ;
That my feet may be merciful,
So that I may hurry to assist my
neighbor,
Overcoming my own fatigue and
weariness . . . ;
That my heart may be merciful,
So that I myself may feel all the
sufferings of my neighbor.

SISTER FAUSTINA KOWALSKA, **Diary,** 163

A NOTE FROM THE TRANSLATOR

———

The texts in this collection are excerpts from homilies, speeches, meetings, addresses, and exhortations delivered by Pope Francis since 2013, some of which have been translated into English and are in the Vatican archives. Where possible, I have turned to these for inspiration and as resources.

I have used the New American Bible, Revised Edition, for all Bible references and lines quoted directly.

I would like to especially thank editor Mika Kasuga for her spirit of collaboration and professionalism.

ABOUT THE AUTHOR

———

JORGE MARIO BERGOGLIO was born in
Buenos Aires on December 17, 1936.
On March 13, 2013, he became
the Bishop of Rome and the 266th
Pope of the Catholic Church.

@Pontifex

ABOUT THE TRANSLATOR

———

Oonagh Stransky's first translation of Pope Francis, **The Name of God Is Mercy,** was published by Random House in 2016. She has also translated Roberto Saviano, Pier Paolo Pasolini, Giuseppe Pontiggia, Carlo Lucarelli, and others. She currently lives in Tuscany.

oonaghstransky.com

LIKE WHAT YOU'VE READ?

If you enjoyed this large print edition of
HAPPINESS IN THIS LIFE,
don't miss this bestseller by Pope Francis,
also available in large print.

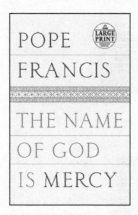

The Name of God Is Mercy
(paperback)
978-0-7352-0976-3
($26.00/$34.00C)

Large print books are available wherever books
are sold and at many local libraries.

All prices are subject to change.
Check with your local retailer for current
pricing and availability. For more information
on these and other large print titles, visit:
www.penguinrandomhouse.com/large-print-format-books

21982318416454